MARKETS AND THE MEDIA

Competition, Regulation and the Interests of Consumers

M.E. Beesley • Dan Goyder
Malcolm J. Matson • David Sawers
William B. Shew and Irwin M. Stelzer

Introduced and edited by
Professor M. E. Beesley

IEA

Institute of Economic Affairs

1996

First published in March 1996

by

THE INSTITUTE OF ECONOMIC AFFAIRS
2 Lord North Street, Westminster, London, SW1P 3LB

IEA Readings 43

ISSN 0305-814X

ISBN 0-255 36378-8

Cover design by David Lucas

Printed in Great Britain by
Bourne Press, Bournemouth, Dorset
Text set in Times Roman 11 on 12 point

CONTENTS

FOREWORD

One of the main concerns of IEA authors is the growth of 'regulation'. Governments, faced with problems which elicit public concern, are all too ready to pass restrictive legislation, establish supervisory committees and commissions, or pass difficult issues to regulators of particular sectors of the economy. Each act may appear worthy and designed to protect the public. But, in the course of time, the probable outcome is a huge regulatory edifice, involving massive compliance costs for firms and individuals. Even more important, it is likely to strike at the roots of economic change by severely hindering entrepreneurship.

The 'media' industries in all their forms are favoured candidates for regulation. Governments seem unwilling to let markets in media work, claiming 'imperfections' and 'failures' which require regulation.

But what substance is there in these claims? To what extent is regulation feasible, given that technological advance is blurring the dividing lines among different forms of media? And are there such problems in the media – for example, concentrations of power through dominant owners – that market processes cannot be trusted to protect consumers?

The aim of *Readings 43*, edited by Michael Beesley, is to explore such questions. Professor Beesley introduces the volume, summarising and commenting on the views of the other contributors. His paper is followed by four chapters which deal with specific issues in media regulation – copyright by Dan Goyder, digital technology and its implications by Malcolm Matson, the future of public service broadcasting by David Sawers, and concentration and diversity by William Shew and Irwin Stelzer.

As in all IEA publications, the views expressed in Readings 43 are those of the authors, not of the Institute (which has no corporate view), its Trustees, Advisers or Directors. It is published as a contribution to the intense public debate about the extent to which media regulation is justified.

February 1996

COLIN ROBINSON
Editorial Director, Institute of Economic Affairs;
Professor of Economics, University of Surrey

THE AUTHORS

Michael Beesley is a founding Professor of Economics, now Emeritus, at the London Business School. Lecturer in Commerce at the University of Birmingham, then Reader in Economics at the LSE, he became the Department of Transport's Chief Economist for a spell in the 1960s. His recent work has centred on the issues of deregulation and privatisation in telecoms, transport, water and electricity, and he is currently Economic Adviser to OFGAS and OFFER. He started a Small Business Unit at the School, a focus for entrepreneurship.

His independent economic study of *Liberalisation of the Use of British Telecommunications' Network* was published in April 1981 by HMSO and he has since been active as an advisor to the Government in telecoms, the deregulation of buses and the privatisation of the water industry. For the IEA, of which he is a Managing Trustee, he wrote (with Bruce Laidlaw) *The Future of Telecommunications* (Research Monograph 42, 1989) and (with S.C. Littlechild) 'The Regulation of Privatised Monopolies in the United Kingdom', in *Regulators and the Market* (IEA Readings No.35, 1991). He has edited all four of the previous volumes in this lecture series, the fourth of which, *Utility Regulation: Challenge and Response*, was published as IEA Readings No.42 by the IEA in association with the LBS in June 1995.

He was appointed CBE in the Birthday Honours List, 1985; and he became Director of the PhD programme in the same year. In 1988 he became a member of the Monopolies and Mergers Commission.

Dan Goyder has been a solicitor with a special interest in competition law for over 30 years. He studied US anti-trust law as a Harkness Fellow at the Harvard Law School in 1962 and (with Sir Alan Neale) co-authored the third edition of Neale's well-known *The Anti-trust Laws of the USA* (Cambridge University Press, 1981). After nearly 20 years in full-time professional practice, first in London and then in Ipswich, he became a part-time member of the Monopolies and Mergers Commission (MMC) in 1980, later becoming one of its Deputy Chairmen in 1991. At the MMC he has participated in a number of references involving copyright issues, including Ford Body Panels (1985), Collective Licensing (1988), Recorded Music (1994) and, most recently, Performing Rights Society (1996). He was awarded the CBE in the 1996 New Year's Honours. He is also a Visiting Professor in Law at King's College, London, and at the University of Essex, and is the author of *EC Competition Law* (2nd edition Oxford University Press, 1992).

Malcolm J. Matson is one of the UK's leading entrepreneurs in the converging infomatics world of telecommunications, computing and television. A graduate of the University of Nottingham, he also gained an MBA from the Harvard Business School. He is a Fellow of the Institute of Management. In the early 1980s he was a pioneer of the UK Cable-TV industry, and was promoter of the first broadband cable operator in the UK to become operational, in Aberdeen. He subsequently sold all his interests in the cable-TV industry to Pacific Telesis. Based on his earlier work as a Winston Churchill Fellow, he developed new concepts for the *fast-moving consumer information* (FMCI) industry and in 1985 was the first person to argue for the concept of *regulated open access* – segregating infrastructure from service provision in the new media industries. In 1989 he founded City of London Telecommunications (COLT) which has become Europe's first all-fibre public telecommunications network. He sold the company to a US investor in 1993 and is now involved in various new initiatives in the information industry which will further lower the barriers to market entry, promote competition and increase consumer choice.

David Sawers is a writer and consultant who specialises in industrial economics. He spent 18 years as an economist in the government service, and has also worked as a journalist and an academic. His major publications are (with John Jewkes and Richard Stillerman) *The Sources of Invention* (1958), a classic study of industrial innovation, and (with Ronald Miller) *The Technical Development of Modern Aviation* (1968), a study of innovation in the aircraft industry. For the IEA he has written, with Wilfred Altman and Denis Thomas, *TV – From Monopoly to Competition – and Back?* (Hobart Paper 15, Revised Edition 1962), *Competition in the Air* (Research Monograph 41, 1987), and *Should the Taxpayer Support the Arts?* (Current Controversies No. 10, 1993).

William B. Shew is a Visiting Scholar at the American Enterprise Institute for Public Policy Research. Following graduate school at the University of Chicago, he taught economics at the University of London. Later, he became a Vice-President of National Economic

Research Associates, a Director of Putnam, Hayes & Bartlett, and Director of Economic Studies at Arthur Andersen. His research has centred broadly on the economics of industrial organisation and market regulation.

His writings on the economics of telecommunications and the media have appeared in numerous journals and books. He has been a consultant to a broad range of public- and private-sector organisations which in Britain include OFTEL, News International, BT and the BBC. He is currently completing a book on how cellular telephone service prices have been affected by regulation and competition, and is beginning research on European barriers to trade in cultural goods.

Irwin M. Stelzer is Director of Regulatory Policy Studies at the American Enterprise Institute, where he studies economic and regulatory policy issues. He is US economic and political columnist for *The Sunday Times* (London) and *The Courier Mail* (Australia), a member of the Publication Committee of *The Public Interest*, and an Honorary Fellow of the Centre for Socio-Legal Studies, Wolfson College, Oxford.

Dr Stelzer founded National Economic Research Associates, Inc. (NERA) in 1961 and served as its President until a few years after its sale in 1983 to Marsh & McLennan. He has also been a Managing Director of the investment banking firm of Rothschild Inc., and Director of the Energy and Environmental Policy Center at Harvard University.

Dr Stelzer has written and lectured on economic and policy developments in the United States and Britain, particularly as they relate to privatisation and competition policy. He is the author of *Selected Antitrust Cases: Landmark Decisions* (7th edition, 1986), and co-author of *The Antitrust Laws: A Primer*, as well as articles for business, professional and popular journals, including *Commentary* and *The Public Interest*. He is consultant to NewsCorp.

Dr Stelzer received his Bachelor and Master of Arts degrees from New York University and his Doctorate in Economics from Cornell University. He is a member of Phi Beta Kappa.

1

MEDIA CONCENTRATION AND DIVERSITY

M.E. Beesley
London Business School

Introduction

CONCERN FOR CONCENTRATION OF MEDIA OWNERSHIP, and devising rules to deal with it to lessen perceived threats to the public interest, have been long-running themes in UK competition policy.

In contrast to the treatment of mergers in industry at large, the Fair Trading Act 1973 contains specific interpretations of the public interest in newspaper cases: such mergers have been subject to automatic referrals to the Monopolies and Mergers Commission (MMC) since 1973. In May 1995, the Government's White Paper on Media Ownership concluded that 'to preserve the diversity of the broadcast and press media in the UK', there is a 'continuing case for specific regulations governing Media Ownership beyond those which are applied by the general competition law' while proposing some liberalisation of existing ownership rules 'both within and across different media sectors' in the context of extended regulation. The Government is contemplating abolishing 'the existing structure of detailed rules', substituting a set of triggers on ownership levels in the 'media market' as a whole, and sector triggers, which when actually or prospectively exceeded would mean the merger would be 'subject to approval by an independent media regulator' to determine 'the public interest'.[1] Thus, 'in the long term' the special treatment of newspaper mergers in UK law would be extended, in modified form, to other media. A separate Quango might be established alongside the other 'UK authorities', or incorporated in them.

---

[1] *Media Ownership*, Cm.2872, London: HMSO, 1995, pp.1, 2.

In the light of the long history of UK competition policy cases, including the cases on newspaper mergers dealt with by the MMC, one might have expected such important proposals to have been accompanied by an analysis of why present concentration in media ownership and increases in it do represent a threat to 'the public interest'. The MMC, in newspaper mergers, has frequently made judgements about that interest. These may be summed up as the advantages of any prospective economies versus threats to the accurate reporting and presentation of views, and to the diversity of views on offer. MMC has also commented on aspects of market conduct, for example, in its reports on *Television Broadcasting Services* (Cm.2035, 1992) and, in response to a reference under the Broadcasting Act of 1990, networking arrangements (*Channel 3 Networking Arrangements*, April 1993). However, since there have been no monopoly (as opposed to merger) references under the 1973 Fair Trading Act, MMC has not reviewed the fundamental underpinnings of power presumptively exercised, and the recent White Paper certainly does not do so either. Moreover, as the other contributors to this *IEA Readings* amply attest, there is good reason to doubt whether there really *is* an issue about media concentration; if there is, it may well be due *to* regulation, not to the lack of it.

This chapter begins by putting the issues in the framework of analysing suspected monopoly power. The practical question facing all governments, or their competitive policy agents such as OFT and MMC, is: What is the gain, if any, from a new rule or a rule change in terms of the applicable public interest criteria to be set against the cost, if any, also associated with the change. With respect to media ownership the procedure should be to assess the significance of proposed ownership changes in the light of underlying barriers to entry. Do these inhibit challenge? How may a change of rules be devised to affect the position beneficially? If action is found to be desirable, the 'change in the rules' can be directed *either* to affecting the conduct of the players, *or*, more fundamentally, to altering existing entry conditions. In the choice between means to the desired end, the power of competent existing competition authorities is highly relevant. If they are perceived to be inadequate, there is a case to legislate afresh.

Ownership concerns property rights. In the case at hand, 'media' means the transmission and receipt of written or spoken words, pictures and music, which is of central concern to the sought-after diversity in the generation of rival views and access to them. (I include music as an important vehicle of persuasion.) The 'media industry' or industries consist of a chain of production, at each level of which property rights are held. Proceeding down the chain, the principal levels are:

- *Copyright holders* of the property rights which are required to create and maintain personal incentives to invest time in developing new ideas;

- *Publishers*, including record companies, and makers of presentations or programmes, who are responsible for gathering and converting the views expressed to widely assimilable forms, or formats. There is a close link with:

- *Delivery systems*, which provide the means to reach audiences – for example, by hard copy, satellite, wires, telecommunications network or cable TV;

- *Receptors* – notably radios, TV sets, telephones and other means – needed by audiences to select among and respond to the views, including 'entertainment' as well as 'serious' productions.

Are there now significant barriers to entry at one or more levels? If there are, competition may be inhibited by vertical ownership. Otherwise, with no significant barriers at one horizontal level, observed vertical integration is due to economies in transactions. In themselves, such economies are rare enough to constitute an independent competition inhibitor.

The above formulation poses the question in terms of what competition is now possible. It outlines the *potential* for challenge. There is also a second question: How do the incumbent property-right owners *now* stand in relation to this potential? Inherited market power is counteracted only with a lag, even if entry is now free. Is there a reason for concern that powerful incumbents, if any, can delay entry for a significant period? If underlying entry conditions are likely to become less hostile to newcomers, there is less concern about present ownership and vice versa.

So the question whether a change in the rules will be beneficial is not only one of deciding whether or not entry is now, or is becoming, freer. If current entry conditions are favourable to newcomers, there is a strong presumption not only in favour of avoiding future interference, but also of dismantling regulation. But if current concentration is high, the large incumbent has incentives to use high market share to put further obstacles in the way of newcomers, so intervention may be justified. The distinction between newcomers' and the incumbent's positions thus turns on conditions of entry which are common to all market participants, and on the particular advantages of incumbency to generate barriers. But even where there is a 'dominant' incumbent now, one must be careful not to read too much into the present state of concentration. Market positions crumble much faster then is usually predicted, especially where technology is rapidly changing. However, government-based barriers to entry may not be so readily challengeable.

Entry Conditions

Our contributors throw considerable light on the significance of entry conditions at the different ownership levels.

New Ideas: The Incentives

At the first level (investing time in producing and developing new ideas), diversity and challenge in intellectual products depend on the motives of the producers. In part, the inducement to such producers is to be heard, and in part economic. Rewards in the form of widespread access to the ideas and views put forward, in whatever format they are expressed, normally go hand in hand with greater remuneration. Copyright is the traditional vehicle to ensure the originator duly gets the monetary rewards. **Dan Goyder** points out (Chapter 2) that, as means of communicating ideas have proliferated, so has protection for the 'effort invested in the creative act'. The range of material protected has increased, notably in computer software and data bases. The degree of protection afforded to literary work by the longest running regulation has markedly increased. UK law, in contrast to EC and US law, has also avoided making protection a function of judgements about 'intrinsic work in', or 'merit of', the 'creative act'. Clearly there is, as he shows, some danger that adoption of such rules will enhance this implicit censorship. But he also illustrates the tendency to reaffirm the rights of the original creator. And he shows the tendency to limit the manner in which a party further down the chain of production can build on the original rights to benefit from their purchase.

That there must be some exemption from competitive forces in order to generate remuneration (in the form of a 'quasi-rent', as economists term it) is widely agreed, and so is the proposition that exemption should be limited in the interests of diffusing the results of the 'creative act'. Hence, for example, patent protection which lasts only for a term of years, and the adoption of compulsory licensing procedures. There are very few 'barriers to entry' to creation itself, though there may be limits to the reservoir of creative talent because, for example, of the quality of early education and training. Since protection of the act of creation has, in general, increased, both by extension of rights and more effective means of collecting dues (as in performing rights), as Goyder shows, inducements to entry at this level have been improved, and there is little reason to fear any regression in the future.

A specific problem with media industries is that the means to realise the intellectual quasi-rents from creative acts depend extensively on the property rights held at the next level of production – the newspaper proprietors, record companies, radio and TV programme producers – all of which, to varying degrees, provide the means of dissemination and act as the effective gatekeepers of ideas. It is surely no accident, as Goyder points out, that the original 'Statute of Anne' of 1709 was propagated by publishers, not by their authors, though the latter were presumably content to see their intellectual returns increased. So the 'creative' person's practical course is either to agree to an agency relationship with the disseminator or to turn the quasi-rents into paid employment (for example, by becoming a journalist). Publishers have used the legitimacy of creativity to pursue their own search for further profit, from restrictions in book-selling. It is at the gatekeeper level that the contrasting public interest in both the protection of 'creative acts' and in competition to broaden dissemination tends to appear.

Goyder shows the ebb and flow of this conflict, in which rules about the balance to be struck are being worked out in a way reminiscent of older battles in another intellectual property rights area, that of patents. What matters more in the present context is what barriers to entry exist at the level of the producer. If the gatekeeping function is difficult to enter, there is a threat to diversity in dissemination of ideas.

Producers of Formats and Transmission

It is difficult to detect in any of the principal producing media types – newspapers, films, television and radio presentations – serious entry barriers stemming from the economics of production.

The most significant potential barriers are property rights giving control over the supply of factors of production and distribution and the size of economies of scale or scope, relative to the prospective market sizes. In newspapers, the succession of MMC merger cases referred to later reveals that entry to newspapers is not inhibited from the supply side. Printing is highly competitive, and whether national or regional newspapers are at issue, cheap access to localised markets is possible from any given production location. The traditional inhibitions on free entry upstream in labour supply have been undermined. In producing material to be transmitted by radio, television or films, the requisite techniques are freely available. Anyone with the ability to persuade capital suppliers can attempt to make output which will attract enough takers to pay back the funds. Economies of scale or scope are very small; they may indeed be negative, as the success of shoestring productions against the failures of attempted blockbuster productions shows. The MMC's report on Compact Discs[2] demonstrated the process by which risk capital is invested in production in advance against the hope of a large, if highly uncertain, return. It also found that a rather high concentration amongst the companies providing the downstream opportunities for marketing did not dull the competitive processes in production. Despite the persistence of artists' practice in assigning copyright to the record-making companies, returns to the artists with the better track records have tended, over time, to yield larger rents to them and to their partners in the creative act.

Traditionally, ownership links with the next level of property rights (delivery systems) has given rise to the perception that entry is difficult at the production stage. For the first 50 years or so of UK broadcasting and world-wide film making, integration ruled. The perception that integration is necessary is now, **Malcolm Matson** tells us (Chapter 3), mistaken. But, at present, entry to terrestrial and non-terrestrial transmission of radio and television is limited. The reasons – and more important, the future prospects for entry – exercise Matson and **Shew** and **Stelzer** (Chapter 5).

Matson points out that in telecoms and radio, the supply of spectrum relative to the technical means to use it, originally created strict rationing and associated licensing and incumbent property rights. But technological development has dramatically eased the problem. He also implies that with these 'wireless' processes the cost of dispersed rather than central despatch to serve the given market has fallen sharply. The prospect is for high frequency radio transmissions to become more economically feasible, even for such large users of capacity as colour TV. Presumably, rival networks built up with small-scale units for the most local distribution will become possible, perhaps borrowing from other technologies for the higher level links in the hierarchy.

---

[2] MMC, *Supply of Recorded Music*, Cm.2599, London: HMSO, June 1994.

Matson also stresses two-way flow use of the low frequency spectrum. Traditionally, radio and television (and newspapers) are means of communication from the few (gatekeepers) to the many (the rest of us). The costs of one-way have been far lower than those of two-way communication. Two-way capability affects the outcome in policy terms in at least two significant ways. *First*, if 'we' can return our own messages, we are enfranchised more effectively. *Second*, two-way capacity undermines the control of a given network. Erstwhile passive receivers can choose the destination and even the routeing of messages. In telecoms, where two-way communication is of the essence, this means the hierarchical, star-like system of communication, with the central owner/operator deciding on switching and routeing, becomes a more totally interconnected system with switching and routeing decided anywhere. The required logistics of operation no longer support the property rights of the network owner.

The prospect of challenge to existing network owners has also intrigued other observers of telecoms policy. In telephony, the most solid base for monopoly power has always been – and still is – ownership of the local telephone loop. Anyone proposing to enter the telecoms business against the established network must be able to offer, from the start, access to all connected to that network. The UK has, by common consent, the most freely entered telecoms market in the world. But 97 per cent of all calls still use BT's network, because of its ownership of near-universal call delivery in particular. The confrontation of a 'free' entry policy and the incumbent position centres on the interconnect problem – the terms on which the incumbent's network can be used: the conflict is even now being argued as an outcome of Oftel's December 1994 paper on the future 'Framework for Competition'.[3]

Developments in Spectrum Use

With respect to developments in spectrum use, were all players convinced that the alternative radio means provides an imminent threat of effective, nationwide local entry in telecoms, telecom policy could proceed on the assumption that competition will soon rule. Sub-conflicts, like the position of a national wire-based player such as Mercury, and the terms of competition between cable TV providers and BT, would then become much simpler to solve. However, uncertainty about the scope of radio-based competition, its further technical

[3] *A Framework for Effective Competition: A Consultative Document*, Oftel, December 1994.

development and cost, mean it is officially judged that this simplifying assumption cannot at present safely be made.

As regards media policy, the prospects of telephone entry via radio are also important in determining whether the assumption can be made that rival radio transmission means are easily entered. Telephone experience is useful because the incentive to test its feasibility is so high, and entrants are free to do so. The way competition has developed in telecoms has meant that entrants have so far not sought to substitute for 'plain old telephone service' to fixed points, even though that still far outweighs, by an immense proportion, the more sophisticated add-on services which have proliferated in recent years. They have instead chosen to compete in mobile telecoms, requiring the capacity to hand on calls from cell to cell at high cost. Entrants' choices may change, depending on prospective profits. It is probably true, however, that the contribution short wave radio can make to building alternative media networks for two-way communication is too limited now to make a substantial difference to media supply.

Meanwhile, the impact of telephone policy on access to the media has not been helpful. The first effective rival entrants to the local loop were cable TV companies, sufficiently important now to be a focus of concern in BT's latest annual report.[4] Their entry was at least greatly helped, and perhaps entirely conditional upon, regulatory rules which bar BT from transmitting TV programmes, while cable operators could offer telephone service over their own newly-laid wires. If there were no impediments of this kind, no doubt the entry of BT would mean more competition. But the other side of the coin is that producing entry against an incumbent itself requires a likelihood of profit. This in turn requires that the entrant has his own form of at least temporary protection against competition. In the cable companies' case this took the form of banning BT from replying by entering TV programme delivery. This particular form of protection may well have been too drastic and prolonged. Nevertheless, without some form of shelter, entry does not occur. The incumbent's position *vis-à-vis* entry, and vice versa, has to be considered explicitly.

Importance of Optical Fibre

While impediments to entering broadcasting transmission are declining, Matson clearly thinks the most important contribution to

[4] 'The main threat continues to be posed by other network operators [meaning Mercury, principally] and the growing number of cable companies, the majority of which receive financial backing from abroad.' (BT *Annual Report 1995*, p.8.)

freer markets will be the potential of optical fibre in terrestrial supply. This has always been regarded as a field in which there are great advantages to a first mover in supplying networks. As Martin Cave notes:

> '...traditional terrestrial delivery offers unlimited economies of scale (a zero marginal cost of extra viewers) within the reception area; it also offers an economy of scope (falling average cost per channel as the number of channels increases), through joint use of transmission facilities.'

The same has been held to apply in cable provision. Though each household must have its own connection,

> 'it is highly plausible that the cost per channel of constructing a cable system would decline as the number of channels increased, especially as the cost of laying a cable system is independent of the number of channels carried'.[5]

With optical fibre as the cable, there is a vast extension of the capacity to carry messages at near zero cost; the initial cost of laying down is further spread. Even where applied to 'one-to-many' distribution (as in TV) and thus not requiring two-way capability, optical fibre, once laid and connected, offers a substantial challenge to traditional terrestrial broadcasting. Often the vision goes further, to think of a dominating, national broadband information highway, on which all will depend. But there are two reasons why what are essentially economics of system fill (adding extra customers) would not lead to natural monopoly problems – and to the allied question of which property interest gets the first mover advantages – thus foreclosing further entry.

First, how rapidly do average costs decline as customers are added? Virtually every economic activity has economies of scale and scope. The real question is how important they are in relation to potential market size at a given price, which must include all the necessary value-added items. It is significant, as Cave reports:

> 'the fullest study of US cable systems (in 1981) found that while the costs of operating a system did indeed increase less than proportionately to the number of homes passed, it was rather small'.[6]

---

[5] Martin Cave, 'An Introduction to Television Economics', in Gordon Hughes and David Vines (eds.), *Deregulation and the Future of Commercial Television*, Hume Paper No.12, Edinburgh: David Hume Institute, 1989, pp.13, 14.

[6] *Ibid.*, p.14.

The advantages lay, rather, in falling costs per customer as more services are packaged and sold per customer. In other words, the conditions for increasing returns lie elsewhere than in transmission, a result which Cave found rather surprising, but which is surely better viewed as a part of Matson's vision of a very large variety of services subject to competing suppliers over the network.

The competing potential cost functions for the rival technologies – such as conventional and optical cabling, terrestrial transmission for radio and TV, two-way radio networks, satellite supply – appear never to have been systematically explored. The reason is partly the sheer complexity of modelling cost with appropriate market scale and value assumption built in as a feedback, as must be done in assessing business viability. This, no doubt, helps explain why those in a position to build the dominant first-mover position in optical fibre have not taken the plunge. BT, for example, has been notably equivocal, very largely because of its huge stake in conventional wires, which has drawn it towards the alternative strategy of digital compression (giving conventional capacity extended application).

Second, and more fundamentally, from the point of view of costs, the question is the absolute size of the transmission element in the average final price of output. If infinite capacity is cheap, then very many will supply it. Hence the proliferation of optical fibre networks in the USA for telephony, particularly in densely populated areas, but also in long-distance provision now entry is much freer in telecoms. Feasibility of entry depends, rather, on the problem of wayleaves – how to avoid having to create them. When the issue of entry of competing networks in UK telephony first arose in the 1980s, it was widely felt the incumbent's possession of all suitable telecoms wayleaves might cause problems. Would it not therefore be necessary to force BT to share? (BT itself, of course, sturdily refused to incur 'the technical risk' to its own system if such interlopers were allowed.) In the mid-1990s this problem seems to have solved itself. Even in longer distance transmission, Energis boasts of its low-cost optical fibre network, courtesy of National Grid's pylons. Wayleave rents are settled now by potential competition, not the exercise of exclusive rights. In practice, much of the attractive market (in urbanised areas, where the bulk of the population resides) has a rich set of utility wayleaves already, which can much reduce overall costs, even if not serving one's new network wholly.

Receptors

Removal of one potential bottleneck to entry serves to highlight the next bottleneck. The leading candidate seems to lie on the border between property rights in transmission and those in receptors (the fourth level identified above, p.3). It is the encryption required to be incorporated in receivers if exclusivity of reception-transmitted information is to be preserved. This, in turn, is a necessary condition for payments to be exacted from TV viewers for transmitted programmes.

Since much of the diversity which is sought in media policy hinges on providing alternatives to transmission not paid for directly by viewers, for instance, by advertising, this appears an important issue. But it is so principally because 'free' consumption of programmes at the point of viewing – either from the BBC or from backing by TV advertising – happens to have come first. Pay-as-you-view or subscription TV has still to arrive. By contrast, in newspapers, freely entered and open to competition, the paid-for instrument came first; then absorbing advertising lowered the price; then, finally, free newspapers funded entirely by advertisements entered, and are now able to give at least some additional diversity. All this happened without appearing, at any one point, to be a 'problem'. However, technical advance in newspapers is not likely to inhibit competition whereas there is some fear that encryption may do so. Shew and Stelzer raise the problem and Goyder's findings are also relevant.

A particular encryption device can become a source of restraint on rival entry, first by establishing the right to prevent copying and second by combination with a distribution system which promises first-mover advantage. The combined effect critically depends on how far rival encryption systems, which do not infringe original rights, can be substituted at similar cost. Goyder's discussion of developments in computer software copyright protection indicates that recent developments in EC law have substantially strengthened such rights; no doubt the same would be held were encryption rights to be tested. A potential policy problem is that such rights are deemed industrial property. Instead of falling into that category of intellectual property rights (such as patents) where monopoly rights are modified by explicit limitations, for example on duration and exercise, they are held without restriction as to their commercial negotiation.[7]

[7] A similar position is emerging in the UK with respect to the Trade Marks Act 1994, intended to align UK policy with European, which has, in effect, strengthened Trade Marks as industrial

However, Shew and Stelzer are reassuring. Not only is present encryption supply 'highly competitive' but in the example of Videocrypt, the 'dominant' analogue standard in the UK, complaints are not about refusal to supply, but about the price of acquisition, which does not appear sufficient to inhibit rival satellite channels from using it. Furthermore, imminent use of digital encryption will not create substitute market power; the rival potential systems are many. The prices charged, even by a very limited number of successful suppliers, will not seriously affect the price of the final customer's receptor. Thus there seems no reason to intervene in the exercise of the property rights involved. Specifically, there is no case for granting monopoly and then applying rules for commercial use, as in patent law, because the required quasi-rents can be generated without such intervention, and rivals will limit their significance. Nor is there a case for using the general pro-competition regulatory mechanism which, as Goyder illustrates, is deemed necessary in analogous situations. At the level of receptors, policy can assume there is no important constraint on rivalry.

This review of the several levels of production indicates that, looking forward, there is little threat of damage to accurate presentation of rival views or their diversity, from commercial constraints on entry. Had the authors of the Media Ownership White Paper undertaken such a review, it would, of course, have been far more exhaustive than is possible here; potential means to create a future 'natural monopoly' problem might have been detected, unlikely as that may seem. More likely, present constraints on entry would have been revealed as the regulatory devices themselves, as in the restriction of the numbers of TV channels and the division of the country into franchise TV areas. These devices, our contributors imply, were means to deal with real or imagined past problems. They are no longer needed.

Are Incumbents a Problem?

Even though the future appears potentially highly competitive, there may be fears that strong present players, reflected in a substantial concentration level, may threaten policy objectives, and that higher ownership concentration in the future must be avoided. The rationale is that, in particular, a powerful incumbent might be able to build upon existing market share to create new barriers to entry in the future,

---

property rights, while ignoring the question of whether there should be an analogy with the patent law's limitations on these rights.

postponing the benefits of rival production and diversity. Incumbents, through their share of the market, will also enjoy an asymmetry of information about markets (present customers) which can be protected by appeal to commercial confidentiality. A more likely reason for concern about concentration is probably the political need to recognise incumbents as claiming special consideration, because of the costs of change. For either, or both reasons, economic or political problems in the transition to competition may be deemed to exist, requiring special regulatory attention.

The economic arguments do not seem well-founded with respect to television, radio and newspapers. In telecoms, there was, and may still be, a stronger case for pro-competitive regulation. But since the speed of arrival of competition is a matter on which different opinions can legitimately be held, there is always a difficult choice to be made. The bold course is to deregulate, and leave subsequent market relations to be dealt with by general competition law. A second course is to accept that existing regulations do deal with entry restrictions, and to attempt to ease entry nevertheless. A third course is to ignore underlying barriers to entry and to devise new rules to add to the old.

Shew and Stelzer take the second line, when they embrace the idea of auctioning existing spectrum, to organise competition for the scarce 'slots'. They describe this bidding as potentially 'the greatest fillip to competition' in broadcasting, to embrace actual as well as potential broadcasters. If it can be effectively conducted – which, given US experience in the cable TV industries, is uncertain – auctioning would certainly transfer monopoly profit to the auctioneer (the UK government in the case at hand). But such an auction would not only perpetuate the myth, if myth it really be, of scarcity; it would do nothing directly to attack the diversity problem. It would merely substitute a different set of broadcasters. There is, however, a more fundamental objection to auctions in the UK case, namely that because of the special status of the principal incumbent, the BBC, there would be no 'level playing field' among bidders with, for example, similar commercial pressures and bankruptcy constraints. As argued below, problems posed by the BBC, if any, must be attacked directly.

The Government's White Paper on Media Ownership[8] would add to regulation. It is regrettable it did not try to justify extended regulation by analysing underlying entry conditions. Because it failed to do so, it

[8] *Media Ownership. The Government's Proposal*, Cm.872, London: HMSO, May 1995.

is not surprising that it did not embrace a strong deregulation line. But, in order to develop the argument, it is useful to accept its premise that new rules to trigger regulatory action are needed to safeguard diversity. Do the White Paper's proposals promise effective action?

The White Paper focuses on market shares above which a regulator must 'assess' the public interest, whether the level is reached already or by 'proposals for merger or acquisition'.[9] The market shares for triggering intervention are defined by a mixture of shares in media as a whole (defined as television, press and radio) and shares of these sectors individually. The triggers for the media sector as a whole (embracing all three) are defined as 10 per cent of the UK market, or 20 per cent of a geographical market embracing all three; 20 per cent of an individual sector – meaning it seems the UK as a whole – is also a trigger. Thus 'in the long term' the media will be incorporated into the body of UK competition law as it affects monopoly and merger. There may or may not be a specialist regulator: one option is to extend the OFT's remit.

UK Competition Law Mechanisms

Effective action will depend partly on these triggers – how to define them specifically, and who they will catch – and partly on what happens to the 'assessment' when made. On the measurement of media markets, the White Paper does not back a particular measure. However, its candidates[10] are dealt with by Shew and Stelzer who argue convincingly for the 'hours of use or audience time of the media', as the White Paper puts it, as the correct measure. They effectively dispose of the White Paper's rival suggestions, advertising or consumer expenditure, and the British Media Group's approach.

Shew and Stelzer's results clearly set out the incumbent problem, measured relevantly over the media as a whole. Their results may be put in MMC terms as a conventional four-firm concentration ratio of about 61 per cent or, as in more relevant recent MMC practice, a Herfindahl index[11] of about 2,100. This would indeed be sufficient to 'cause concern' in the typical MMC monopoly inquiry and exceeds most analysts' trigger levels. But the significant point is the influence

---

[9] *Ibid.*, p.22.

[10] *Ibid.*, para.6.13.

[11] A concentration measure which sums squares of market shares, thus giving greater weight to the size distribution of firms as a whole.

on the concentration measure of the largest 'firm' – the BBC, with 44 per cent of the 'market'.[12] Were it not for the BBC, there would be no concern at all over concentration (as conventionally measured). The next biggest firm, Carlton TV, has only 6·9 per cent of the market. So, the answer to the question of who the proposals are designed to catch is, in part, easily answered. The BBC, the only significant source of concentration, is excluded as outside the private sector. I come back to this important point later. But, meanwhile, it is useful to pursue the White Paper's position in its own terms.

Data underlying Shew and Stelzer's Table 2 (below, p.134) show that only in (national) newspapers does one group have more than 20 per cent of the audience. News Corporation (embracing *The Sun*, *The Times*, *News of the World* and *The Sunday Times*) has 37 per cent, and the Mirror Group (*Daily Mirror*, *Daily Record*, *Sunday Mirror*, *Sunday Record*, *The People*, *The Independent* and *Independent on Sunday*) has 26 per cent. Excluding the BBC, the largest share in television is Channel 4's 10 per cent, and in radio Capital's 10 per cent.

The immediate main target of the White Paper appears to be the two large newspaper groups which, in effect, are put on notice that further mergers in the sector or integration into other media will be scrutinised. The BBC, because it is in the public sector, is not affected by the proposed triggers. TV rivals have too small a national share to be caught by that trigger, but might qualify under the geographical rule which is obviously defined (albeit tentatively) with the existing regional TV licences in mind.

The package, by raising the possibility of an 'assessment' and refusal, targets newspaper entrepreneurs, inhibiting their freedom to buy into major TV stations. Lesser cross-media moves will be able to proceed without this inhibitor. Shew and Stelzer's work demonstrates that News International has only 3·4 per cent of the media market and the Mirror Group 2 per cent. Their possible integration into TV must, therefore, be intended to be caught by the White Paper's provision that the regulator would have to 'assess' existing holdings above the thresholds, where the relevant threshold could be deemed to be the individual media 'sector'.

The concern about a maximum of (say) 7 per cent of the national media market (for example, Carlton) being added to the 3·4 per cent or less held by a big newspaper group may seem odd in normal UK

---

[12] See Shew and Stelzer, below, Table 3, p.135.

monopoly control terms, especially when entry conditions are becoming freer. But how are the rules, in the context of traditional UK competition law, likely to operate? Specifically, how far will they, in practice, inhibit concentration change? The rules must be assumed to operate rather as in the past. They are an extension of the special treatment for newspaper mergers, where we have 20 years' experience and 31 cases to draw upon.

The Newspaper Experience

The record does little to explain how the leading newspaper groups – which are the principal targets for the new triggers – have reached their present market shares. If the control is competent to catch all significant cases, the implication is clearly that the growth of these groups must have been almost entirely due to their success in building up against competition without merger. What the control did catch was not the evolution of concentration at the national level, but many cases of shifts of ownership of regional and local newspapers.

The important point about a control is its limits – what does it not permit? Four cases of the 31 were found to be against the public interest.[13] In these four, as with all the others, the criteria considered were effects on accurate presentation of news and free expression of opinion; on employment and efficiency; on competition; and on concentration of ownership. The central grounds for rejection were, in effect, the issue of diversity, as reflected in concentration of ownership. The cases in the 1980s were strongly influenced by concerns of the 1977 Royal Commission on the Press, about local and regional concentration.[14] The nearest MMC came to a *per se* rule, expressing its priorities amongst the criteria, was in the West Somerset case:

---

[13] The four were:

1. *West Somerset Free Press and Bristol United Press Ltd.*, HC 546 (1979-80), London: HMSO, 1980.
2. *Century Newspapers Ltd. and Thomson Regional Newspapers Ltd.*, Cm.677, London: HMSO, 1989.
3. *Mr David Sullivan and Bristol Evening Post plc*, Cm.1083, London: HMSO, 1990.
4. *Daily Mail and General Trust plc and T. Bailey Forman Ltd.*, Cm.2693, London: HMSO, 1994.

[14] Cmnd.6180, July 1977.

> 'there are *prima facie* reasons on public interest grounds against any individual acquisition of a local newspaper which carry the process of concentration further'.[15]

Two of the later cases took a less open and shut line, but still focused on the diversity rather than the competitive aspects of concentration. The very high levels of concentration found did not inhibit competition, but did threaten diversity. As the latest case put it:

> 'although there will be little effect, at least in the short term, on readers' choice of newspapers...there will be a significant increase in the concentration of ownership of newspapers in an important region of the country'.[16]

In three other cases there was a conditional judgement requiring conditions to be met for approval.[17] Two of these again concerned local concentration; certain local titles had to be dropped from the merger. The other case should be of great interest to those who believe internal arrangements within companies can surmount the common ownership threat.[18] The majority of the group considering the case worked out a very elaborate set of rules to be attached to the consent centring on independent directors as observers.[19] Dr R.L. Marshall's note of dissent is a classic rebuttal.[20]

The newspaper cases indicate that the diversity issue will be prominent among the MMC's criteria, but that the Commission mechanism will be at best a mild deterrent, to rein in further shifts in an already extremely high level of concentration. Concentration ratios of

---

[15] MMC, *op. cit.*, para.7.18.

[16] *Daily Mail & T. Bailey Forman, op. cit.*, p.17.

[17] The three cases were:

1. *The Observer and George Outram & Co. Ltd.*, HC 378 (1980-81), London: HMSO, 1981.
2. *The Berrow's Organisation Ltd. and Reed International Ltd.*, Cmnd.8337, London: HMSO, 1981.
3. *T.R. Beckett Ltd. and EMAP plc*, Cm.623, London: HMSO, 1989.

[18] *The Observer and George Outram & Co. Ltd., op. cit.*

[19] *Ibid.*, pp.75-77.

[20] *Ibid.*, p.78.

40 per cent to 100 per cent were frequently encountered.[21] The overwhelming impression from the 31 cases is that MMC judgements had little impact on diversity.

UK Competition Law Practice

Moreover, even when the MMC has reported, whether there is consequent action depends on the Secretary of State of the day. The implications of this, and the degrees of freedom a Secretary of State has to avoid a reference in the first place, were well illustrated in the last newspaper merger case of 1994.[22] Though MMC made an adverse finding, and held that no conditions could be devised to mitigate the effects of the proposed transfers of ownership, the Secretary of State allowed the transfer, praying in aid sections of the 1973 Act which allow mergers or transfers of assets if he is satisfied there is a danger of a newspaper's failing because of its economic difficulties. This recourse is one of the main reasons why mergers involving major independent but financially insecure titles have seldom been referred. The White Paper on Ownership proposals will, in effect, embrace this aspect of the system.

That a regulatory system works as a minor brake on shifts of ownership is, in view of the findings about entry conditions, something of a relief, though it is unnecessarily expensive and raises questions about the accountability of politicians.[23] But a major doubt remains: the failure of present UK competition law and related administrative procedures to provide a means by which the principal assumption which should underly regulation of the media (namely, the conditions of entry) can be revisited and, if necessary, acted upon.

Because of its continued focus on acquisitions and mergers, serious consideration of what underlies market power may well continue to be bypassed. That is the province of the monopoly reference; in the case of newspapers no such reference has been made because, if it is recognised at all, the ground is deemed adequately covered by the merger provisions. True, the Director General of Fair Trading came close to having the issue opened by referring 'the supply of National

[21] This is not surprising if one is prepared – as some group members of MMC will always be – to take a focus as local as Eastbourne or Seaford (as in the T.R. Beckett case, *op. cit.*, para 6.23).

[22] *Daily Mail and General Trust and T. Bailey Forman Ltd., op. cit.*

[23] A theme explored by C.D. Foster in *Utility Regulation: Challenge and Response*, IEA Readings No.42, London: Institute of Economic Affairs, 1995, pp.135-39.

Newspapers',[24] as noticed by Shew and Stelzer. But this was not an inquiry into concentration of newspapers *per se*: it considered 'supply from publishers to wholesalers' and from 'wholesalers to retailers'. It thus considered newspaper distribution, and was directed to a particular aspect of conduct ('practices in the supply of newspapers'). The MMC had to be satisfied as to concentration to required levels at newspaper publishing and wholesaler levels, and thus was led to downplay Shew and Stelzer's relevant points about what the 'market' to which newspaper ownership levels apply really is.

The White Paper on Media Ownership[25] refers to an intention to ask 'the regulator' to assess existing holdings above the thresholds as well as mergers or acquisitions. As explained earlier, this could provide the basis for assessing a large newspaper's proposal to acquire a major TV station. It could also be read as inferring that, in contrast to past practice, a fundamental monopoly inquiry would, if necessary, be mounted. But the power has always formally been available. The point of the White Paper is to bring non-newspaper media into the control. That the 1973 Act has not been used, for example, to explore TV concentration, is simply because when the BBC is easily the market leader and is exempt from such an inquiry, there is no point (and dubious legitimacy) in trying to refer much lesser concentrations, even though they might at some point technically themselves comprise a 'complex monopoly'. As things stand and are to be carried forward, we may never see a straightforward monopoly reference, even of newspapers, unencumbered by the rest of the mechanism.

But again, undue alarm about this is lessened because in newspapers, as in other media, underlying competitive prospects are found to be good. Three practices were complained of: newspaper owners setting cover prices, setting retail margins, and exclusive supply arrangements. However, the MMC felt it could not propose means to make competition more effective, except for a reform (minor in the context of a highly perishable commodity), namely, giving retailers the right to move supplies between outlets and to sell on to other retailers.[26] The central point is that the practices, which supported wholesale and retail margins to limited numbers of handlers in the past, are far less effective

24 Cm.2422, December 1993.

25 *Op. cit.*, p.22.

26 Cm.2422, *op. cit.*, paras.11, 117.

nowadays in stopping entry. So far as newspaper owners themselves are concerned, no-one doubted their vigorous competition.

The BBC and Media Concentration

If there is an incumbent problem in a world of potentially free entry it must, as Shew and Stelzer demonstrate, first and foremost concern the BBC. In this respect, *Media Ownership* is a Hamlet without the Prince. The BBC appears but fleetingly in it. It says:

> 'Public Service Broadcasters will be included in market share calculations, but will be excluded from regulation because the government already has direct control over their ownership' (p.6).

In other words, we (the government) will be responsible for the BBC's conduct, not the regulatory mechanism. The BBC is also mentioned (at page 20) as 'to be consulted over proposals to raise equity ceilings between an independent producer and a broadcaster'. The BBC is easily the biggest producer, so the government's own incumbent is to be given at least rights of veto. How this is consistent, if it is, with encouraging 'joint ventures between public service broadcasters and private companies' (p.21) is not shown. The reason for this conspicuous offstage player is, of course, that the BBC charter is being renegotiated. *Media Ownership* has to be read in concert with July 1994's White Paper on the future of the BBC.[27]

Future Public Policy Towards the BBC

Policy towards the BBC is **David Sawers**'s principal concern (Chapter 4). For him the central problem is how to end public broadcasting. He proposes that the BBC's licence fee should, as soon as the new Charter would permit, be run down, to a fixed timetable. The BBC must then substitute advertising, sponsorship, pay-as-you-view or subscription fees to survive. I thoroughly agree with David's insistence on consumer sovereignty and his strictures on the pretensions of paternalism; and he shares the other contributors' view about the capacity of markets to respond competitively.

However, the two White Papers suggest that the notion of continuing the fee is now firmly decided upon by this Government for the immediate future, with some effort over time to substitute alternative

---

[27] *The Future of the BBC*, Cm.2621, London: HMSO, 1994.

means of funding the continuing 'public broadcaster'. 'If the BBC services are to remain widely accessible, there is no practical alternative to the licence fee before the end of the century, and possibly for some years after' (p.31). Though the BBC has failed so far in providing commercial encrypted subscription services, 'there may be other opportunities' for making money commercially. There is no intention to allow the BBC to be a competitor for TV advertising. Much attention is devoted to how to revamp the payment of licence fees (needless to say, a change of government would be highly unlikely to modify the basic position). Even more significantly, the Government used the 'recent developments in broadcasting internationally' in which 'new multi-media organisations are linking programme making, the provision of broadcasting services and the means of distributing them, whether by conventional terrestrial broadcasting or by cable and satellite' (p.26) to throw doubt on its own 1989 policy of privatising the BBC's transmission services. Here it feebly concludes 'it is not clear whether the audio-visual industry will be more closely integrated or more fragmented in the longer term' (p.26).

A cynic might well conclude that since conditions for entry into conventional transmission's rivals are now easier, the smaller prospective quasi-rents have dampened the resolve to privatise! But there may, belatedly, be a recognition that direct government rules to regulate entry are superfluous in emerging technical conditions; the market will be more freely entered but the Government has decided that the BBC must be maintained as a large public sector operator. That would explain the 1995 White Paper's silence on the BBC.[28]

Retaining a large public sector operator is not consistent with allowing competition law to rule. To apply the full ambit of the 1973 Act, implies making the BBC subject to normal monopoly inquiries. Along with other public corporations, the BBC is exempt from them, though subject, as all public organisations now are, to criticism and comment on their conduct (for example, via the Competition Act 1980). Rather like the Post Office, the BBC has claims on public approval which severely limit the present Government's scope for manoeuvre in fundamental matters like privatisation and phasing out of particular public bodies. It seems worthwhile, therefore, to consider what issues arise when free entry is combined with a large, publicly funded operator, bearing in mind the principal policy objectives of

[28] *Media Ownership*, Cm.2422, *op. cit.*

generation and dissemination of new ideas and enhancing diversity and access.

The prospects are for a considerable period in which the BBC will maintain its output, from a set income capped by the RPI change, substituting over time some of that revenue by commercial partnership ventures, where these can be struck. Substitution will be limited because of the inherent difficulties of allocating risk.[29] Also (regrettably in my view), BBC production of TV and radio programmes will remain integrated with transmission. My regret is because of the opportunity lost to expose the transmission to capital market disciplines via privatisation, rather than the fear from effects on entry conditions which, as argued earlier, will become easier.[30]

In any case, it is doubtful whether hiving off transmission would greatly diminish the scale of the BBC's activity. Because the BBC is under no obligation to approach the standards of disclosure required nowadays of leading private sector firms, it is impossible to tell how much the BBC puts into the stages of production, the programmes, and how much into transmission. Even the biggest single source of information, the Peacock Committee on Financing the BBC,[31] contains no means to decide this. But the 1994 BBC White Paper[32] does say: 'The BBC has some 700 engineers employed on operating and maintaining its television and radio transmitters' (p.26). This was some 20 per cent of the BBC's current full-time employment in 1994. The Peacock Committee gives, but for as long ago as December 1978,

---

[29] The Treasury's idea of a collaboration is to remove all the risk onto the commercial partners that are paying for the higher risk they take, whereas commercial interests want the assurance of public sector backing to reduce their risk, without sacrificing profit.

[30] The line taken here contrasts strongly with those who believe – wrongly in my view – that somehow one can eat one's cake (a publicly governed BBC) and have it (an expanding, commercially active BBC competing on level terms with the private sector). The basic idea is that if one splits up the BBC, so that the publicly funded BBC is the sole shareholder of subsidiaries with the normal accounting requirements for reporting, that this isolates the latter satisfactorily. This is mistaken; a 100 per cent shareholder carries the basic bankruptcy risk, and all the problems of isolation remain. Proposals like this are normally coupled with a far too optimistic view of how governance mechanisms in the 'public' part of the BBC can be made more open to public influence than now, and, at the same time, maintain the public/private internal split. For a contrary view, see Richard Collins and James Purnell, 'The Future of the BBC: Commerce, Consumers and Governance', Institute for Public Policy Research Discussion Paper, 1995.

[31] Cmnd.9824, 1986.

[32] Cm.2621, *op. cit.*

percentage breakdowns of 'total expenditure' (Table 6.9). This gives 57·3 per cent to staff costs, 24·9 per cent to 'programme allowances' (artists' fees, and so on), 3·3 per cent to the Performing Rights Society and the 'House Orchestra', and the rest (13·5 per cent) to various overheads. If we allocate 25 per cent of staff to transmission activities, the rest to programmes and apportion overheads according to relative staff costs, we arrive at an overall split of roughly 18:82 per cent transmission to programme production. If these proportions are even approximately valid, and hold, the BBC would still be easily the largest single force in producing what is seen and heard in the UK, even if transmission *were* privatised.

Significance of BBC's Continuance as Large-Scale Subsidised Operator

What is the significance of the large-scale subsidised activity for a diversity of views, and the range and quality of programmes? Views on the BBC's output have been strongly influenced by two perceptions. *First*, it is commonly held that faced with competition, the BBC is motivated to cling to market shares as a target, because of the link between that and its probability of retaining or increasing fees. *Second*, it is committed to raising the quality of output. This was, for example, the position taken by Hughes and Vines.[33] Much of the heat in discussions before and after the Peacock Committee was concerned with the BBC dilemma – how far to pursue quality at the risk of losing support for its preferred subsidised operation. What the Government has now done is to weaken the first motive and, therefore, the constraint on the BBC's behaviour. Normally, with public organisations, some *ad hoc* ministerial objectives fill the vacuum in giving the organisation direction, especially if under financial pressure from the Treasury. Where there is no such pressure the organisation substitutes its own objectives. So, in public UK utilities before privatisation, because they were no threat to the public purse, what dominated production decisions was pursuit of technical excellence allied to views of what the balance of the public interest required.

BBC's 'Morrisonian View of Public Enterprise'

The BBC is the epitome of this Morrisonian view of a public enterprise – indeed, it is the last great bulwark of this 1920s idea. And its charter,

[33] *Op. cit.*, p.49.

when finally renewed, is most unlikely to shift this view. The current intention in the White Paper to make clearer distinctions between management and Board functions will make it more business-like. There is, for example, an intention to give the board responsibility for appointing the Director General.[34] Otherwise, the emphasis is on retaining the governors' 'due impartiality'. The BBC's independence 'should be recognised in the new Agreement (effectively its licence), with the expectation that the Board of Governors and the BBC managers will take account of Parliamentary comments on the BBC's activities' (p.45). As for selection of those to whom the public interest will be entrusted, the governors, there are still in effect to be '12 good men [and women] and true': 'The Government will continue to look for people with varied experience and backgrounds'. There will be no Select Committee approval of appointees – this is 'too political'. To all intents and purposes, there will still be a Morrisonian devolution of the public interest to a set of guardians. The outcome will certainly be welcomed by creators of programmes, innovative or otherwise; they will have captive transmission, not greatly subject to commercial pressures, as their show case. We can expect little threat to programme diversity, and possibly the contrary, from this prospect, for several reasons.

The usual worries about large subsidised activities are, *first*, that they represent opportunities for effective price cutting on the outputs they choose, to the detriment of competition, and, *second*, that they represent unfair competition in the attraction of inputs, notably productive talent in this case. As to price cutting, that there is, in some sense, a weak bankruptcy constraint in the BBC's case cannot be denied. However, since the total budget is to be so circumscribed, there cannot be 'a long-purse' strategy to knock out competition unless a particular line of output is targeted. Then one might indeed encounter the problem which followed deregulation of the long-distance bus industry (alone) in 1980, but which left the National Bus Company to pursue whatever tactics it liked. (It duly went for retaining market share in inter-city buses regardless of profit, because profits from most other activities, themselves heavily subsidised, were not affected by deregulation.) But one cannot see agreement in the BBC to a particular target area, to be funded at everyone else's expense. The governors would not find this consistent with their public duties. Probably more

[34] White Paper on the Future of the BBC, Cm.2621, *op. cit.*, p.53.

important, there would be debilitating strife among the professional programme-makers within the BBC.

As to 'unfair' buying of talent, of course, the principal effect of such large subsidy is (artificially) to increase the overall available supply of talent. This may be regrettable waste, but it is hardly likely to make it too costly to enter into competition for the talent. In sum, this particularly large incumbent is unlikely to be a serious threat to diversity; the contrary is more likely. The increasing opportunity for entry at each productive level will make it more and more a large-scale subsidised cultural centre, with an enviable ability to air its own productions. The natural question to ask is whether this should be recognised explicitly – for example, by merging the BBC licence fee with the rest of cultural funds. The Peacock Committee considered briefly the possibility of the BBC's relying on a national lottery for funds, but concluded that the latter was not likely to be successful enough. In 1996, this opinion might be revisited! But the die is probably cast.

The foregoing paragraphs pursue a different line from Sawers'. They do not deny it would be better if his solution to the BBC's problem were to be adopted – in effect, one of privatisation over time. I would have added, following his line, that there should be immediate privatisation of transmission and at least structural separation of television production and radio down to the requisite of financial reportage, an obligation which should be put upon the BBC immediately. But, given the Government's 'vacuous' White Paper, as he calls it, we are probably obliged to consider the BBC's status as given in the short term. The logic of freer entry implies that even as a large subsidised organisation, it must adapt: it can no longer drive the market. Its significance will be more and more as an independent supplier of programmes *not* subject to the demands of the *existing* market-place. It will be a major source of innovative programming and views, some of which will strike subsequent market support, possibly large-scale support. This may well be an extravagant way of subsidising cultural diversity and, as Sawers argues, be redundant in those terms. But it is unlikely to be a commercial menace, if governments follow the 1994 White Paper's intentions. Rather, the danger lies in failing to dismantle present regulations because of the Government's reluctance to confront *Media Ownership* with *The Future of the BBC*. On this, much hinges on what is being inserted in the new 1996 Charter, at the time of writing known only to insiders.

Summary

To summarise, the argument of this chapter is that concern about media concentration is misplaced unless there are substantial barriers to entry. An examination of the four levels of production involved – using material from the other chapters in this volume – shows clear evidence of weakening constraints to entry, likely to gather momentum because of technological change and entrepreneurial response. It follows that concern about movements towards integration across the media is similarly misplaced.

It is logical to consider the existing incumbent position (the degree of concentration now) as an independent factor because of the possibility that strong incumbents could develop fresh barriers to entry on the basis of present market shares. This is equally improbable now, but there remains the need for a mechanism to review this possibility at intervals in the future. The most cogent reasons why the 1995 White Paper on Media Ownership fails to be relevant is its neglect of basic economic issues, and even more important, its failure to confront the commercial implications of the BBC's being easily the largest player in the media scene (a failure found also in the 1994 White Paper on the BBC's future).[35]

The 1995 White Paper proposes, in the long term, a substantial prolongation and elaboration of regulation, involving the present UK competition law process not, as economic logic suggests, seeking a way forward in dismantling regulations as no longer needed. Even arguing from its own premise of the need for such elaboration, its proposals are likely to be ineffective. There is a long and neglected history of newspaper merger cases, which suggests little substantial effect on concentration in either direction and, more significant, too much dependence on ministerial decisions to allow cases to go forward to, or take action following upon, MMC reports. Essentially this position is to be carried forward in the proposed regulatory régime.

Moreover, the proposals do not provide for an effective confrontation of future technical constraints on entry, should these emerge. In this the

---

[35] Two further official statements relevant to this paper appeared in 1995. In July, Oftel produced its response to the December 1994 Consultative Document, *Effective Competition: Framework for Action*, Oftel, July 1995; and in August, the Government's Proposals on Digital Terrestrial Broadcasting (Cm.2946) were published. They do nothing to meet the needs for analysis argued for here. The context taken is still that of the 1994 White Papers. The tendency to look for more elaborate control mechanisms to go alongside increased competition is reinforced, particularly in the case of Oftel.

White Paper merely reflects the general failure of UK competition law to provide properly for incumbent market power. As I have argued elsewhere, this should be overhauled to drop attempts to prescribe and regulate that power only when it is manifest, as UK policy now does, in favour of measures which will greatly increase the prospective costs of exercising monopoly power, including far more reliance on private actions to recover damages for losses incurred, which could well be punitive.[36]

But a focus on regulating the private sector in the media industries misses the main point about concentration – the very large share held by the BBC, whose future as a subsidised, large-scale producer is underwritten in the 1994 White Paper. This prospect does not, as many have argued, pose an economic threat to other players. I do not disagree with Sawers's preferred treatment of the BBC, of a timed transition to private funding; indeed I would urge, in that context, immediate reforms such as the divestment of transmission and far more stringent financial reporting standards. But if the Government persists with its 1994 line (and there is no sign yet of a divergence in favour of privatisation), the practical focus of further policy reform should be the present Government-inspired impediments to entry, notably in licensing networks of all disciplines including telephony, radio and TV channels.

[36] M.E. Beesley, 'Abuse of Monopoly Power', in *Regulating Utilities: The Way Forward*, IEA Readings No.41, London: Institute of Economic Affairs, 1994, pp.139-60.

2

COPYRIGHT, COMPETITION AND THE MEDIA*

Dan Goyder

Solicitor, Visiting Professor in Law, King's College London, and at the University of Essex; a Deputy Chairman of the Monopolies and Mergers Commission

Introduction

IT IS AN ESSENTIAL FEATURE OF LAW and the legal system to be able to adapt in response to the pressure of change. Sometimes this adaptation is by formal substantive enactment, prepared by Governments and approved by legislatures; at other times it is the outcome of decided cases in the courts, handled by imaginative judges moulding existing jurisprudence successfully to cope with the demands of the new situation. Change may come in a political, social, economic, cultural or technological form or from a combination of some or all of these factors.

In recent years the enormous changes in the media, largely driven by the communications and computer network revolutions, have raised very significant new problems for the law. The central issue has been the problem of reconciling on a equitable and workable basis the different interests of those who control, work for or benefit from the media as well as of those who provide the creative input, in an unpredictable world where few of the old certainties can be relied upon and where even such familiar categories as data, text, video and audio may well become irretrievably intermingled.[1]

Communication through the media has two important strands, which could briefly be described respectively as informational and cultural.

* The views expressed here are personal to the author and do not represent those of any official body.

[1] N. Higham, 'New Challenges of Digitalisation', *European Intellectual Property Review*, Vol.10, 1993, p.355.

There are always prosaic details that need to be conveyed, such as the national or local news, the weather forecast for next Friday or the announcement of new governmental regulations; but at the other extreme there is the excitement of the latest 'No.1 hit' pop song or the premiere of an eagerly awaited new symphony. So long as the channels available for both kinds of communication were themselves limited, as also their potential audience, the protective function of the law for its content could remain simple. As, however, the scope, variety and technical complexity of these channels (which we often now loosely refer to as 'the media') has grown so the legal protection required has become more complex. Moreover, whether the form and extent of protection for 'information' alone should be as extensive as for the 'cultural' has recently become a keen subject of debate and legal measure.

The instinct to create is an inherent feature of human personality. Societies of the past, whether the Athenian civilisation of the 5th century BC or the Netherlands in its Golden Age from 1540 to 1640, are largely judged by the intensity, variety and genius of the literary, artistic and philosophical creativity they displayed. Any product of the creative mind, however, is as vulnerable (and perhaps more so) to the threat of unfair appropriation as any tangible item of property. Its legal protection by the concept of copyright is therefore essential to the welfare of society. Copyright, though an apparently simple idea, is actually a highly flexible mechanism which has proved adaptable to changing circumstances. It no longer provides merely a protection against deliberate 'copying' of another's labour but is now a multi-faceted concept applicable in a wide variety of different situations. Once entirely a matter for individual enforcement by the copyright owner it is now increasingly and necessarily enforced collectively, in situations where the individual owner cannot in practice monitor his own rights. Once mainly national and territorial in scope, much of copyright is now also the subject of international treaty as well as of directives of the European Community.

The Origins of Copyright – Publishing and Bookselling

We do not know whether medieval scribes were ever in the habit of unfairly copying each other's illustrated manuscripts.[2] It seems likely

---

2 There is a story from the 6th century AD that Columba of Iona visited his former teacher Finian in Ireland and made an unauthorised copy of a psalm book: when Finian discovered this the resulting dispute was referred to King Diarmint of Tara who ruled in favour of Finian on grounds of basic equity! ('To every cow her young cow, that is her calf, and to every book its

that disputes over ownership did occasionally arise, but the first well-documented use of copyright seems to be linked with the development of a regular commercial bookselling and publishing trade in the United Kingdom during the 16th century. This was a right claimed at that time primarily not by the authors themselves but by booksellers and publishers, who organised themselves into the Stationers' Company, with the aid of a charter from Queen Mary in 1557, and claimed protection against those who might unfairly seek to reproduce copies of their wares without permission. This practice of copyright had fallen into disuse by the end of the 17th century but was then replaced by the 'Statute of Anne' in 1709.[3] Originally simply a negative right to prevent someone else from profiting by making a copy of one's own original work, the content of the right has grown considerably over the subsequent three centuries. Numerous 'neighbouring rights', such as those required to protect films and recorded music, have also developed. UK legislation on the topic has itself grown steadily in scope and complexity as the coverage of the right has itself widened. This has been matched in virtually every other developed country in the world, with the support of a number of international treaties whose past and present rôle in the regulation of copyright is mentioned below.

The gulf between the Statute of Anne and the current consolidating UK statute, the Copyright, Designs and Patents Act 1988 ('the 1988 Act') is therefore enormous. The original coverage provided for books and original literary work has now extended *inter alia* to newspapers, sound recordings, photographs and a number of other creative forms. The length for which protection has been given has risen from originally 14 years to 28 and later 42, with a further extension to the author's lifetime plus seven years; the current UK protection is for life plus 50 years and by EU Directive[4] this has now been increased throughout the EU to life plus 70 years. The original Statute of Anne had a mere handful of clauses; the 1988 Act has 306, together with eight full-length schedules, the whole occupying 238 pages of small print. The Act itself has already been substantially amended as a result

---

transcript.') (See the *International Encyclopedia of Communications*, Vol.1, pp.411-22, published by Oxford University Press and University of Pennsylvania, 1989.)

[3] The next country to provide similar protection for authors was Denmark in 1741. Of even greater significance was the French law introduced by Napoleon in 1793.

[4] See note 12 (below, p.36).

of EC directives[5] subsequently adopted (more are in the pipeline) and also by the introduction of the compulsory licence for the publication of broadcasting schedules contained in the Broadcasting Act 1990.

The philosophical basis of copyright in common law jurisdictions, notably the UK, Ireland, and in the countries of the 'Old Commonwealth', such as Australia and New Zealand, has been protection of the effort invested in the creative act, a recognition primarily of the labour undertaken by the author and perhaps to a rather lesser degree of his or her skill. A necessary consequence of this approach is that a fairly low level of originality can legitimately find protection in copyright legislation. In other words, copyright protection extends in principle as much to the collection or 'compilation' of information (which will normally involve at least a modicum of labour and expenditure) as to artistic, cultural and creative invention. What is worth copying is normally deemed to be worth legal protection.

By contrast, the law in most Continental European countries places the emphasis on the individual intellectual and creative contribution of the author. The '*droit d'auteur*' places the emphasis on the entitlement of the author to be associated with his work as well as his 'moral right' not to have it disfigured or mutilated, metaphorically or literally, by third parties. Legal protection therefore has, in these jurisdictions, tended to emphasise the importance of the creative and cultural, rather than the informational, aspects of copyright. Nevertheless, for many years these two divergent philosophies of copyright have co-existed. The influence over the last four decades of the Treaty of Rome has, however, been in general to strengthen the influence of the civil law approach. In Articles 36 and 222[6] it acknowledges that the importance to the European Community of free movement of goods between member-states cannot be in total disregard of the rights of the owners of 'industrial and commercial property' or of the rules in member-states governing the system of property ownership, including intellectual property.

---

5 See note 12.

6 Article 36 provides a number of grounds on which prohibitions on the free movement of goods can be justified by member-states, including 'the protection of industrial and commercial property', provided it does not involve arbitrary discrimination or a disguised restriction on trade between member-states. Article 222 preserves the rights of member-states with regard to their national systems of property ownership. The reconciliation of these two Articles with the requirements in Article 30 for free movement of goods between member-states is the subject of extensive European Court of Justice case law.

Changes in Copyright Protection for the Media

There have been a number of changes in the nature of copyright protection for the media over recent years which have largely reflected the unprecedented growth in the commercial and technical developments described elsewhere in this volume. Four major areas of development can be identified:

- The range of material protected has tended to increase, especially in the area of technical and informational material such as computer programmes (software) and databases. The protection given to such new forms of copyright often contains special rules appropriate to the new areas protected; these rules themselves seek to balance the protection of creators with the broader needs of their customers. There are also always those who seek to expand (not necessarily with success) the scope of copyright, for example, by extending its protection to some forms of creation not previously covered, such as published financial information and the format of television programmes.

- The emphasis on the enforcement of copyright and the prevention of infringement in neighbouring rights, such as recorded music, in great measure has passed from the individual to the collective, with the development and growth of both national and transnational collecting societies to represent and protect the individual owners (both authors and publishers) of copyright in their hundreds of thousands or even millions worldwide.

- Although copyright remains an intellectual property right which is primarily national and territorially linked, its effective application to a much larger number of countries has now become far more dependent on a framework of international convention, especially the Berne Convention and the recent GATT Treaty.

- Within the European Community, most of the early case law of the European Court of Justice in this area was concerned with patents and trademarks, but in subsequent years copyright too has been the subject of both case law and Community legislative action. Successive directives from the Commission, reached after extensive debates between experts from member-states, have sought to harmonise (that is, impose a greater degree of uniformity on) many aspects of copyright law within the Community. In particular, the

> Community has sought to provide appropriate protection in all member-states for more recent technological developments, so as to prevent uncontrolled copying of these by third parties where this could damage legitimate interests of creators and owners. The rights of owners of copyright have not, however, been treated as absolute, but made conditional upon these rights being exercised in a manner which does not infringe certain provisions of the Treaty of Rome; particularly important are Articles 30 to 36 and 59 dealing with the free movement of goods and services and Articles 85, 86 and 90 dealing with competition. This has brought into sharp focus the conflict between, on the one hand, the requirements of the copyright owner and, on the other, the aims of competition law and policy, both within the Community and at national level.

Each of these four heads is considered in turn.

The Scope of Copyright Protection: EC and US Developments

So long as the focus of copyright protection was on works of individual literary creation the author, as first owner of the copyright, was clearly identifiable as the individual who had written it, or any assignee to whom his or her rights had passed either during his or her lifetime or after death by the laws of succession. Once, however, the categories of work to be protected had themselves expanded, naturally the range of those with a legitimate commercial interest in them also increased. Once, for example, recorded music was covered, not only was the composer of the music and the author of any related verbal content (for instance, the words of a song cycle) to be protected but in addition the performers of the work.

The scope of protection with regard to films has also developed. Under English law copyright belongs to the person responsible for making the necessary arrangements for the making of the film, that is, the producer or the production company. The civil law approach placed greater emphasis on the '*droit d'auteur*', in this case those collectively responsible for the creative input that together enables the film to be produced and shown. Principal among these is the director, who under a recent EC directive is entitled to be treated as an author of the film but with the possibility that other co-authors may also be nominated by individual member-states, including the producer, sound track composer and screen writers.[7]

---

[7] See Article 2, Directive 93/98; see also note 9 (below, p.35).

The current statutory listing of the material considered worthy of protection in the United Kingdom is set out in Section 1 of the 1988 Act and covers:

a) original literary, dramatic, musical or artistic works;
b) sound recordings, films, broadcasts or cable programmes; and
c) typographical arrangements of published editors (though the protection term here is shorter than for normal copyright, being limited to 25 years).[8]

An interesting question has been raised as to the exact scope of even these apparently straightforward definitions. It has long been an accepted doctrine of UK law that a mere idea or concept cannot itself be protected but only its expression in language or in pictorial or other visible form. In the case of *Green v New Zealand Broadcasting Corporation*[9] it was held by the Judicial Committee of the Privy Council that the mere 'format' of a television programme – that is, its main unifying features and characteristics – is not protected under existing copyright law, though apparently in practice payment is often made by producers prepared to acknowledge the commercial value of 'borrowing' a format that has already proved its worth elsewhere. An attempt to have such formats for programmes included in the 1988 Act failed but their potential value has now led the Department of Trade and Industry to raise again, in a published consultative document of May 1994, the possibility of extending UK copyright law to include such programme formats as 'literary or dramatic' works, provided they are both original and sufficiently detailed. *Opportunity Knocks*, which was the subject of the *Green* case, was actually a quiz show, and any extension of copyright law in this direction would benefit a whole variety of programmes in the media, including serials and current affairs productions not currently protected in this way.[10]

The main influence on the expansion of the reach of copyright law, however, has been the activities of the European Commission, which regards the harmonisation of intellectual property rights as an important aspect of the single market. The 1988 EC Green Paper, *Copyright and*

---

[8] Section 15, 1988 Act.

[9] [1989] 2 AER 1056.

[10] The fact that such a proposal has been made for extending the scope of UK copyright does not of course guarantee its adoption.

the Challenge of Technology,[11] contained a general review of the ways in which such harmonisation could benefit media throughout the Community, both by preventing its operating through totally separate national markets and also by making it easier to control piracy. A working programme was produced two years later leading to subsequent enactment of three relevant directives[12] over the period 1991-93.

Protection of copyright has now by directive been extended to two new forms of property. The first is the computer programme, the software vital to the functioning of any computer. The 1988 Act had already recognised in its Section 3(1)(b) that a computer programme was capable of being protected as a literary work by copyright law in the UK. The Directive (91/250),[13] however, goes into considerable further detail in setting out the applicable rules; thus protection applies to the programme provided 'it is original in the sense that it is the author's own intellectual creation'. Since such programmes do not operate normally in isolation but have to have an interface with other programmes, the user of the programme is nonetheless to be entitled to reproduce it and 'translate its contents' so as to be able to use it alongside other programmes. This right of 'decompilation' only applies if there is no other means available of achieving a working interface between the separate programmes and does not extend to authorising the provision of copies of the information produced by the 'decompilation' to third parties whose involvement is not essential to the user's computer operation. Nor does the right apply to simply reproducing the original programme in order to make copies for commercial purposes, as opposed to the legitimate making of such copies for use as back-up in the event of accident to (or loss of) the original programme.

A second directive extended the rights of the holders of copyrights in 'related rights'. These are extensive and cover 'fixation',

---

[11] COM (88) 172, final version dated 2 March 1989.

[12] A directive does not take legal effect within a member-state until implemented by national legislation; failure by a member-state to enact such legislation in time can lead to claims for damages by persons to whom the failure has caused financial loss. The three directives are respectively (1) Directive 91/250 on the Legal Protection of Computer Programmes (adopted 14 May 1991, effective 1 January 1993). (2) Directive 92/100 on Rental and Lending Rights (adopted 19 November 1992, effective 1 July 1994). (3) Directive 93/98 on Term of Protection of Copyright (adopted 29 October 1993, effective 1 July 1995).

[13] Embodied in UK law by SI 1992/3233.

'reproduction', 'broadcasting' and 'distribution' rights.[14] 'Fixation' means the recording in any way of a performance of copyright material in a form so that it is then capable of dissemination in one or more media. 'Reproduction' is the act of dissemination made possible by the original fixation of which 'broadcasting' is one particular example. 'Distribution', on the other hand, relates to the commercial exploitation of the format (such as film print, compact disc, cassette or vinyl record) on which the copyright work has been recorded.

This directive also assists producers of films and sound recordings who are given the right to control not only authorised reproduction of their creations but also to control both rental rights and lending rights for their products. Rental rights comprise the making available of a video or recording for a limited period to a customer on commercial terms, whilst a lending right would cover a non-commercial loan, for example, one made by a public library to a member of the public. Copyright owners of such items are also granted control over 'distribution rights', so that they can control (or prevent altogether) the import into the Community of products by way of parallel import which they have licensed for sale abroad. This right, of course, does not extend to a product which has been legitimately sold or licensed *within the Community itself* by the copyright holder or with his consent. As we shall see below, when examining the way in which free movement of goods is permitted under Article 30 of the Treaty, the rights of the copyright owner himself have to be limited in this respect in order to protect the principle of free movement.

A further directive[15] extends the term of protection for copyright users. In the case of literary, dramatic or musical works (including now also photographs) the period is extended from the life of the author plus 50 years to life plus 70 years, thus bringing the period for the UK into line with the longer periods already in force in Germany. The period of protection for sound recordings and for films is also being equalised at 50 years from the date of their release, already the period provided in the UK.[16] The benefit of such an extension would apply to any author whose works were protected in at least one member-state of the Community at the relevant date of 1 July 1995. Some tricky legal

[14] Directive 92/100: see in particular Articles 6-9.

[15] Directive 93/98. The Directive has been implemented in the UK by SI 3297/1995 ('Duration of Copyright and Rights in Performance Regulations').

[16] Section 13, 1988 Act.

questions will arise in transitional cases where authors have died at or about the end of the Second World War. There is also the consequence that authors or composers who died between 1925 and 1945 will re-enter a second period of copyright protection! There has therefore been some suggestion that the harmonisation in this direction may verge on the over-protective.

A form of property to which the protection of copyright is also to be confirmed by directive[17] is the database – a collection of financial, commercial or historical information arranged and stored electronically and available for consultation 'on line' by subscribers. A key feature of the database is the way the data are organised and arranged by an index and it is this method of selection or organisation chosen by its creator which is protected by the draft Directive. The individual items of information that make up the collection will normally already be protected by conventional copyright, though a further right for its maker to prevent 'unauthorised extraction or reorganisation of the contents' is also given for a period of 15 years. It is significant, however, that the provisions of this Directive may fail to cover some databases that UK law would itself protect by copyright as compilations of information.

Whilst the most extensive developments in limiting the exercise of copyright in databases have thus been in the European Community, the United States itself does show some trend towards limitation of copyright holders' rights in 'informational material'. The well-known *Feist*[18] case, (US Supreme Court, 1991) underlined the importance for the copyright owner of establishing at least a degree of originality for the material sought to be protected. In this case a company called Rural Telephone Service had prepared a telephone directory containing an alphabetical list of names, addresses and numbers. Feist asked to be allowed to use that list in order to produce a larger telephone directory covering the same area as well as neighbouring areas. When Rural refused to provide such a licence Feist nevertheless used the information for the compilation of its own directory.

When Rural then sued Feist for infringement of copyright the issue reached the Supreme Court; it held that factual databases could only be

---

[17] This Directive was finally adopted in February 1996, and has to be implemented in member-states by 1 January 1998. The terms of the final draft of the Directive can be found in OJ/1993 (C308/01).

[18] *Feist Publications v. Rural Telephone Services*, [1991] 111US 1282.

protected by copyright if the selection and arrangement of the relevant facts was original. Mere expenditure of work and labour and even skill on the task was insufficient. In the view of the Supreme Court, copyright

> 'means original...in that the work was independently created by the author (as opposed to being copied from other works) and that it possesses at least some minimal degree of creativity'.

The Court further found that since Rural's alphabetical list could not be described as original, Feist had not infringed copyright by making use of Rural's list in compiling its own directory. The attitude of the USA towards such databases probably falls somewhere between the civil law requirement for both originality and creativity and the UK's concept of the need for protection of work and effort in preparation of such a compilation.

Finally, the exponential development of cable and satellite transmission systems as channels for communication has led to a further directive[19] which governs the control by the author of the communication of his copyright material to the public by satellite; it lays down as a basic principle that the necessary consents have to be given by the copyright owner in the country where the 'uplink' through the satellite is situated. Exceptions are provided, however, for the case where the originating source of the satellite transmission is actually outside the Community, when the rights of the copyright owner in the 'receiving' country are protected.

Collective Licensing

A recent major development in copyright enforcement is the growth in size and importance of collective licensing bodies acting in the interests of individual copyright owners. While the primary concern of an author or newspaper editor or television producer may be negative – to use copyright so as to protect others from appropriating his material – the concern of those, for example, whose talents have enabled the production of records (in whatever format) or the writing of pop songs or other music is for the maximum commercial exploitation of their production, leading to the payment of royalties as well as other financial benefits from the success of their work.

---

[19] Directive 93/83, adopted 27 September 1993, effective 1 January 1995.

Royalties payable to the author of an individual book are relatively simple to collect, at least in the case of copies legitimately published with the author's authority. By contrast, the calculation and monitoring of royalties' payment to performing artists, including both creative writers and musicians, for their work present greater administrative problems. The record company will, of course, normally have contractual obligation to keep details, subject to regular audit, of what has been sold, and therefore of the sums due to the artist under his royalty agreement, once advances for living expenses and recording costs[20] have been 'recouped'. On the other hand, royalties payable for the broadcasting, let alone public performance, of copyright items cannot in practice be effectively monitored by individuals. Indeed, even major companies would have difficulties economically in monitoring the exact claims to payment in respect of each playing of a work by a radio station, discotheque or café, especially since the use may be simply of part or the whole of a single track from a much longer album. Collecting appropriate royalties in one's own country would be difficult enough and to do so for use on a European, let alone a world-wide, basis is likely to be impossible for the individual.

The existence therefore of collective societies is the only feasible way in which such royalties can be collected in an effective and economical way. Their essential functions were described in a report of the Monopolies and Mergers Commission (MMC) published in 1988, as follows:

> 'Collective licensing is adopted everywhere in the world where copyright is enforced. It is long-established (in the United Kingdom since 1914, in some other parts of Europe since the mid-19th century). It is a system under which copyright owners combine to offer use of the works under their control, normally without specific advance consent, against payment of the fees specified and subject to compliance with any other terms of the licence. It offers convenience to users, who are saved the burden of seeking advance consents from rights owners, and convenience to owners, who are saved the labour of identifying the use of copyright, determining tariffs for that use, collecting royalties, distributing the revenue, monitoring the use of copyright material and enforcing copyright. Collective licensing bodies, however, are by their nature monopolistic – indeed, their potential for effectiveness depends in large measure on the extent of their monopoly –

[20] Usually known as A&R advances.

and it is widely accepted that appropriate controls are needed to ensure that they do not abuse their market power.'[21]

In the United Kingdom the longest established collecting society is the Performing Right Society (PRS) which on behalf of authors, composers and publishers licenses the use for public performance and broadcasting of original musical works, and associated literary work; there is also the Mechanical Copyright Protection Society (MCPS) which licenses the mechanical rights, that is, the recording of such works. Acting on behalf of producers of records, cassettes and compact discs, etc., is Phonographic Performance Limited (PPL) which collects royalties for their public performance and broadcasting, whilst Video Performance Limited (VPL) carries out the same functions for videos. Each collecting society has its own set of tariffs which have been negotiated with the relevant representative bodies of users, or in some cases, determined as a result of contested proceedings before the Copyright Tribunal set up under the 1988 Act to have jurisdiction over such collective licensing schemes.[22]

A recent example of this case has been the dispute between broadcasting organisations on the one hand and newspaper proprietors on the other as to the level of royalties to be paid by newspapers for the right to print television and radio schedules for the week ahead under the compulsory licence provided by the 1990 Broadcasting Act.[23] Clearly, the interests of all copyright owners are not identical, and the conflict between the perceived need for an effective monopoly organisation in collecting and allocating royalties and the inherent possibility of abuse of that power has led to a number of cases in the Community which are discussed below.

International Agreements

Copyright is essentially based on national law; the rights it provides are initially inherently territorial and limited in effect to one country. In the

[21] MMC, *Collective licensing of public performance and broadcasting rights in sound recordings*, Cm.530, London: HMSO, December 1988, para.3.4.

[22] See Chapter VII, 1988 Act (Sections 116-135).

[23] Section 176 and Schedule 17. This licence arose as the result of a long and successful campaign by press and magazine proprietors to end the duopoly of TV and broadcasting schedules in the UK by the BBC and ITP through the *Radio Times* and *TV Times* respectively. The *Magill* case referred to later in this chapter is of course concerned with the same issue at the European Community level.

past there has been no universally agreed definition of its scope, nor of the exceptions to that scope. The need to extend the territorial effectiveness of national copyright by way of international treaty led therefore in the later 19th century to the negotiation of the Berne Convention for the 'protection of literary, artistic and scientific works'. The Convention has since been renegotiated at regular intervals to bring in new signatories and to extend its coverage in response to new technical and cultural developments. Whilst valuable, it is far from providing totally comprehensive protection. Under the Paris Act, which is the latest version of the Berne Convention adopted in 1971 and now accepted by just under 100 countries, a number of basic principles have been laid down which bind the signatories, except to the limited extent that some specific derogation is allowed, for example in the case of some less developed countries.

These principles include:

- Basic copyright is affirmed for the author who alone is entitled to authorise reproduction, public performance, broadcasting, translation and adaptation.

- These rights are to be enjoyed without formality, for example, the need to register or deposit copies, and are to last for a minimum period of the author's life plus 50 years.

- The limitations and exceptions permitted to this right are specified, for instance, a compulsory licence of copyright material is only permitted in limited circumstances.

- In addition to the rights set out above, authors are also entitled to 'moral rights' which are concerned with the integrity of the link between the author and his creative output, including the right to be publicly acknowledged as author and not to have their work mutilated or their reputation damaged.

- The principle of national treatment is affirmed, that is, each signatory country must accord to works originating in other Berne Convention countries the same rights that its national law accords to works of its own nationals (although there are a few exceptional cases where reciprocity of treatment is required).

Neither the Berne Convention nor the Universal Copyright Convention, itself an alternative international copyright treaty, deals with sound recordings. For this reason a separate convention was adopted in 1961 known as the Rome Convention for the 'protection of performers and producers of phonograms (i.e. records) and broadcasting organisations'. This sought to lay down equivalent principles for these categories of copyright owner but only with limited success both in terms of the numbers of signatories, currently 40, and in coverage, as it provides a restricted series of rights only. It gives considerable discretion to the signatories as to the obligations they accept for sound recordings and films and provides a minimum term of protection of only 20 years. The Geneva Convention on Phonographs has even more limited scope since it really deals only with the problem of piracy, that is the illegal making of copies of films and recordings.

Dissatisfaction in the USA, in particular with the effectiveness of these existing international agreements, was largely responsible for the GATT multilateral negotiations between 1986 and 1993 including for the first time productive discussion on 'trade related aspects of intellectual property' (TRIPS for convenience). The TRIPS agreements, once they have been fully ratified by all parties, represent real progress by developing countries (albeit under strong pressure from the USA and other 'copyright exporters') in the acceptance of a broad international framework, utilising the existing international agreements but strengthening their application, for the establishment in almost all countries of enforceable intellectual property rights. These include time limits for protection broadly in line with developed country practice; for example, the period for literary and dramatic material is to be at least 50 years and a similar minimum period is provided for performers and producers of recorded music. All participating countries must also provide adequate procedures under their national law for enforcement of the agreed substantive rights.

Conflict Between Copyright and Other Policy Objectives, Notably Competition

The owners of copyright would naturally prefer the specific subject matter of their rights (including the ability to exploit them commercially by the wide variety of methods that current technology makes possible) to be safeguarded, without being subject to control or restriction for the sake of other public policy goals. Unfortunately for them, in some situations the aims of competition policy (as well as other public policy goals) come into opposition with the protection of intellectual property rights, including copyright. No account of the current state of the media and copyright protection therefore would be complete without referring to some of the leading issues and cases that illustrate this conflict.

Since intellectual property rights, by definition, normally provide their owners under national law with a form of monopoly, it is not surprising that competition authorities have had on occasion to seek to resolve the conflicting interests of such owners with the requirements of competition policy when these appear inconsistent. Several references to the MMC under UK competition legislation have involved such issues. Two cases in 1985 raised the question of whether the owners of intellectual property rights could be compelled to grant licences to potential users of those rights. The first involved the Ford Motor Company, which had a practice of not allowing the manufacture by third parties of replacement body panels protected by copyright under the terms of case law in force at the time. Independent suppliers which had pioneered the manufacture of replacement parts for those affected by corrosion were not granted licences for manufacturing such replacement panels even though willing to make payment of a reasonable royalty; this practice was held to be anti-competitive under the 1980 Competition Act.[24] The MMC recommended to the Secretary of State that this practice should be discontinued but, on the basis of the law as it then stood, had no power to make even a recommendation that Ford should grant a licence on reasonable terms to the independent manufacturers. The MMC did, however, suggest that the law should be changed, so that functional items having no design features of an artistic quality should in future cease to be protected by copyright and would simply have the less extensive protection conferred under registered design law. Appropriate legal changes to this effect were included in the 1988 Act which also for the first time gave the Secretary of State powers (following a suitable finding and recommendation from the MMC) to order compulsory licensing when a copyright owner refused to grant licences on reasonable terms to would-be licensees. Any disputes over the terms of such compulsory licences would be referred to the Copyright Tribunal.[25]

---

[24] Sections 2-10 inclusive. The report is published as Cmnd.9437.

[25] See Section 144(3) of the 1988 Act which states that these powers are only to be exercised if the Minister is satisfied that they would not contravene any international agreement to which the UK is a party.

A second case in 1985 concerned the long-running dispute between the BBC and ITP on the one hand and newspaper and magazine publishers on the other over the right to publish programme schedules for the BBC and independent television programmes. It came to a head with the making of a reference by the Director General of Fair Trading to the MMC under the Competition Act 1980. The issue posed was whether the refusal by the broadcasting authorities to license these schedules on a seven-day basis (as opposed simply to making them available for 24 or 48 hours ahead) was anti-competitive and against the public interest. The BBC and ITP's argument was simple. They owned the copyright in the schedule 'compilation' which UK copyright law, with its emphasis on skill and labour rather than on originality, undoubtedly protected and had no legal obligation to license it to others. Their refusal to do so for a seven-day advance period was mainly attributable to the lucrative advertising revenue which the *Radio Times* and *TV Times* could thereby attract, having no UK competitors for publication of the weekly schedules.

The outcome of the reference was a narrow victory by 4 to 3, including the Chairman's casting vote, in favour of the broadcasting authorities. The basis for this decision was that, although the practice of refusing to license was anti-competitive, it was not against the public interest, as the limited licensing terms that the BBC and ITP were offering were themselves reasonable and it was not felt by the majority of the MMC group, if the existing system for licensing the schedules were abandoned, that any replacement would serve the public better. The minority view to the contrary was that the public interest was not served by the public being denied 'the possibility of being offered programmes and information for seven days ahead about all four television channels in a convenient format in a simple publication'.

The apparent victory for the broadcasting organisations was, however, short-lived since the Government subsequently included in the 1990 Broadcasting Act[26] for the first time a right for any 'publisher' to require the provision of information as to the programme schedule and relevant titles in time to enable publication of them in its own product (newspaper or magazine). The royalty payable was to be determined, if in dispute, by the Copyright Tribunal. Whilst this settled the issue in the UK it was also to arise almost simultaneously in the European Community in the famous *Magill* case. This involved the

[26] Section 176 and Schedule 17. The report on this case is published as Cmnd.9614.

radio and television services in Ireland where a publisher of programme information challenged practices similar to those of the BBC and ITV.[27]

The provision of historical online database information was examined in another MMC report[28] published in May 1994 under the monopoly provisions of the Fair Trading Act 1973. One of these scale monopolists, holding more than 25 per cent of the relevant market, was the Financial Times Group Limited which refused to license the contents of *The Financial Times* on its database to those independent 'hosts' who competed with it, and with each other, to provide database services for businesses, academic institutions and individuals. Had a public interest finding been made against *The Financial Times*, a remedy under Section 144 of the 1980 Act would have been possible, leading to compulsory licensing of such material to the hosts. On this occasion, however, the MMC found that *The Financial Times* was entitled to act in this way, since it was neither charging a substantially higher price for its information than the other database competitors nor making excessive profits from this business. Its refusal to grant licences to them was regarded as 'a legitimate competitive action which did not impair competition'. It was relevant also that much of the content of *The Financial Times* database was available from other sources, such as the Stock Exchange and press agencies, whereas of course in the *Radio Times/TV Times* case the seven-day schedules were not available elsewhere in the UK.

Another legal principle which inevitably comes into conflict with copyright is that of freedom of contract. The pop group which attracts the attention of a record company may find that substantial advances are available from the company to pay for the time and resources required for production of its first album on compact disc and cassette. But at the same time it may well find that the *quid pro quo* it must accept is an assignment of its copyright, in all the music contained in the album, to the record company, without any provision for its return at a later date should relationships deteriorate or their agreement terminate for that or any other reason. It is argued by record companies that only by acquiring outright ownership of the copyright material, can

---

[27] The details of the EC case are discussed below: the initial complaint to the European Commission was made in April 1986 but the ECJ's decision on appeal was not given until nine years later!

[28] Cm.2554.

they afford to invest in the creative talent that enables the material to be produced.[29]

If owners of copyright therefore are fully subject to competition legislation in the context of anti-competitive practices, it is nevertheless clear that under the United Kingdom's 1976 Restrictive Trade Practices Act (dealing with agreements rather than practices), the owners of intellectual property rights, including copyright, are treated generously. The *Ravenseft* case[30] dealt with restrictions contained in a lease of commercial premises but the case is accepted in practice by the Office of Fair Trading as applying also to those restrictions maintained in the licences of intellectual property. The heart of that decision is the principle that potential licensees of intellectual property are not normally entitled to any rights at all, except those which the owner/licensor decides to provide. If therefore an owner/licensor places restrictions on the licence so granted covering the copyright material, those restrictions simply limit the terms of the licence, that is, provide the licensee with half a slice of cake instead of a whole slice, and do not thereby place any 'restrictions on the licence' which would require registration under the Act. A large number of specific categories of copyright licence are, moreover, expressly excluded from the 1976 Act by its terms.

By contrast, under EC law, the position of the owner of copyright is less secure and considerably more liable to challenge under principles of competition law. Case law over the last 30 years has seen the gradual development by the European Court of Justice of rules under which potential conflicts between these principles have been reconciled with each other, not always (as we shall see) in a way wholly favourable to the owners of copyright.

The Treaty of Rome and the European Court of Justice: A Summary of Cases

The principal rules contained in the Treaty of Rome which raise these issues are to be found in Article 30 (which prohibits measures having equivalent effects to quantitative restrictions on imports), in Article 85 (prohibiting agreements or concerted practices restrictive of competition within the Common Market), and in Article 86 (prohibiting

[29] See paragraphs 12.96 to 12.114 inclusive in the MMC report on *The Supply of Recorded Music*, Cm.2599, London: HMSO, June 1994.

[30] [1977] 1 AER 47.

an abuse of dominant position within the Common Market). It was inevitable that sooner or later, through use of these Articles, an attempt would be made to limit the freedom of the owners of copyright and other intellectual property rights to exploit their rights. In this chapter, only a brief summary can necessarily be given of a large number of complex cases decided both at the European Court of Justice and, more recently, at the Court of First Instance, also in Luxembourg, often dealing with intellectual property rights other than copyright, such as patents, registered designs and trademarks.

Nevertheless, copyright is fully accepted as 'industrial and commercial property' as defined in Article 36 and its treatment has played an important part in the development of Community law. In a case in 1982 involving the French film producer, Coditel,[31] the European Court of Justice acknowledged that the owners of copyright in films were fully entitled to grant exclusive licences to Belgian distributors without falling within the prohibitory range of Article 85(1), notwithstanding that these licences were exclusive; the special difficulties of obtaining a return on investment in films meant that the use of exclusivity in their distribution could be fully justified in such circumstances. On the other hand, the use of copyright law as a method of supporting a system in West Germany of resale price maintenance on records was defeated in the well-known *DG v. Metro*[32] case in 1971.

The distinction found in these cases under Articles 30-36 relates to the separate concepts of 'existence' and 'exhaustion' of intellectual property rights. The 'existence' of these rights as confirmed by Article 222 protects the initial exploitation of that right by the first sale of a tangible format, for example, of a book or record, from which the owner (author) earns his profit. Once, however, that sale has been made, either by the owner himself or with his consent, then the purchaser, having paid for the item, is free to market it himself in any part of the Community, including in the vendor's own country where otherwise the owner's national copyright would have conferred a monopoly. In Community terminology, the first sale by the copyright owner of such material 'exhausts' his rights and the purchaser cannot thereafter be barred from remarketing the item in the owner's territory. The principle only applies, however, when the consent given by the owner of the property is to a purchaser or licensee within the

---

31 *Coditel v. Cine Vog Films* [no.2], Case 262/81 [1982] ECR 3381 [1983] 1 CMLR 49.

32 Case 78/71, *Deutsche Gramophon v. Metro* [1971] ECR 487: CMLR 631.

Community and does not apply in respect of licensees or purchasers outside it.[33] Nor does it apply when the copyright owner simply licenses the use of his copyright for performance, as in *Coditel*, rather than actually supplying goods, for example, a book or record.

It is also an important element in Community law that domestic copyright legislation must be applied on a basis that does not distinguish between copyright owners on the basis of nationality. Thus, the well-known United Kingdom pop star, Phil Collins, was held by the European Court of Justice to be entitled to the same remedies in Germany to prevent the sale there of 'bootleg recordings' made of a live concert in the USA as if he had been a German national, notwithstanding that under German copyright law his rights as a 'foreigner' were less extensive than those available to a German national – that is, they did not apply to recordings of performances outside Germany. The provisions of the relevant international Convention (the 1961 Rome Convention) allowed its signatories, including Germany, to provide greater protection for its own nationals so long as a minimum standard of protection was given to nationals of other signatory states; Article 7 of the Treaty of Rome, however, sets a higher standard and effectively bars such discrimination between the nationals of member-states in copyright laws.[34]

The application of this basic principle of 'exhaustion of rights' by copyright owners to other situations has had to be worked out in a large number of cases by the EU Courts. It is clear that the 'consent' of the original owner of copyright is not to be presumed if the particular use of the item sold is not one that is protected in the country or original sale. Thus in *Warner Bros v. Christiansen* in 1988,[35] the owner of video cassettes sold in the United Kingdom was able to prevent them from being rented out in Denmark, even though lawfully imported into that country by the original buyer, because the UK law recognised at that time no right in the copyright owner to prevent the hiring out of videos (so that no 'consent' in goods could be deemed to have been given for such activities in Denmark). Similarly in *EMI Electrola v. Patricia*,[36] the European Court held that the consent of the copyright owner could

[33] *EMI Records v. CBS (United Kingdom)*, Case 51/75 [1976] ECR 811: 2 CMLR 235.

[34] Case C92/92, *Collins v. Imtrat* [1993] 3 CMLR 773.

[35] Case 156/86 [1988] ECR 2605: [1990] 2 CMLR 684.

[36] Case 341/87 [1989] ECR 79 2 CMLR 413.

not be assumed in a case where a Cliff Richard album originally sold in Denmark (where it was out of copyright) was then imported into Germany. The first marketing of the record in Germany by the importer from Denmark was not made 'with the consent of the German copyright owner', but by reason merely of the shorter period of protection that the record had obtained in Denmark. In other words, the rights of the copyright owner are only 'exhausted' if the owner can genuinely be said to have given an effective and voluntary consent to the particular use of the relevant item.

Many of the limitations, however, on the right of copyright holders in Community law arise not under Articles 30-36 but under Article 86. In its very first case dealing with Article 86,[37] the European Court in 1968 not surprisingly confirmed that mere ownership of a patent or other intellectual property right cannot be regarded as abusive, regardless of the extent to which its ownership conferred an effective monopoly over the product, in this case a drug. It was likewise believed for a number of years that the owner of an intellectual property right had a complete freedom to refuse to license it. This assumption was, however, challenged in the context of registered design rights in the *Volvo v. Veng*[38] and the *Renault v. Maxicar*[39] cases. In both these cases, car manufacturers had refused to allow third parties to manufacture replacement car parts body panels relying on their protection by registered design rights and were accused by doing so of violating Article 86. There are clearly parallels here with the *Ford* case already described.

The European Court obviously found the prospect of giving a car manufacturer total freedom from any obligation to license replacement parts unattractive, bearing in mind the obvious needs of car owners (especially of older models) to have access to spare parts, such as these panels, at reasonable prices. It therefore held that, although a simple refusal to license would not by itself be an abuse of its dominant position, a refusal could nevertheless be abusive if the circumstances were 'exceptional'. An arbitrary refusal to provide spare parts for independent repairers, or the fixing of spare parts prices at an unfair level, or refusal to produce parts at all for older models still in

---

[37] *Parke Davis v. Probel*, Case 24/67 [1968] ECR 55: CMLR 47.

[38] *Volvo v. Veng*, Case 238/87 [1988] ECR 6211: [1989] 4 CMLR 122.

[39] *Renault v. Maxicar*, Case 53/87 [1988] ECR 6039 [1990] 4 CMLR 265.

circulation would all for this reason constitute an abuse of dominant position.

These cases, although dealing with cars, were thought to contain some uncomfortable messages for both the media and the communications business, as well as for the computer software market. It might mean that users or licensees of software might have in the future the right to demand licences from the owner of the relevant copyright in a programme now protected by EC directive[40] as well as by the 1988 Act. The Software Directive, of course, itself sought to delimit the extent to which licensees were entitled to make copies of computer programmes to utilise their essential content so as to develop other programmes of their own or to ensure comparability at the interface of the licensed programme with other operating programmes. In the Volvo and Renault cases, however, the European Court of Justice did not specify the appropriate remedy for any breach of Article 86: this might have been damages or an order for a compulsory licence, or indeed both.

However, the impact of the Volvo and Renault cases on the media has now been affected by the final outcome of the *Magill*[41] case which, after an initial Commission decision in 1989, moved on to the Court of First Instance (CFI) in 1991 and finally in 1994 to the European Court of Justice, with the final decision of that Court given in April 1995. The facts were simple and have indeed been referred to in substance already in the context of the 1985 MMC inquiry into BBC/ITP (referred to above). The case arose from the desire of Magill, an Irish publisher, to produce seven-day schedules of Irish television and broadcasting programmes which the owners of copyright in those schedules, including Radio Television Eireann, were unwilling to license to him.

The CFI, in upholding the decision of the Commission that broadcasting authorities, by their refusal to license these schedules, were in breach of Article 86, had made clear that it was possible for the owner of copyright or other intellectual property to lose the protection apparently conferred by earlier case law, if it exercised its rights in a manner which did not any longer correspond to the 'essential function

[40] Software Directive no.91/250 (OJ 1991 L 122/42). This is of course secondary legislation whose effect could be overruled or restricted by a decision of the ECJ on the interpretation of a Treaty provision such as Article 86.

[41] *RTE and ITP v. European Commission*, Cases (C241/91P and C242/91P) (published 6 April 1995).

of the property right'. In other words, it was necessary in the course of the Article 86 assessment to look at the reason for which the particular intellectual property right was granted and to ask the question: 'Is this intellectual property right being utilised in a way which goes beyond its proper use, that is, its "essential function"?' The broadcasting authorities had been held by the Court of First Instance to be using their copyright in programme schedules to prevent 'the emergence on the market of a new product, namely a general television magazine likely to compete with its own magazine' and licensing of the press only on a limited basis (for 24-hour schedules),[42] though simultaneously licensing on a weekly basis for publications in other member-states which would not be in direct competition with their own publications. Such a refusal was characterised by the CFI as 'arbitrary, justified neither by the specific demands of the broadcasting sector nor by the particular nature of the magazines publishing TV schedules'.

On appeal, the ruling of the European Court of Justice itself largely supported the CFI's decision, rather than accepting the preference of its Advocate General, Gulmann, for a finding that the refusal to license such rights was justifiable in the absence (in his view) of 'exceptional circumstances'. In contrast, the Court's finding of exceptional circumstances in this case was based on the existence of the following elements:

- The monopoly right of control by RTE over the basic programme information giving them a dominant position, rather than simply ownership of a specific intellectual property right, especially as the information arose as 'the necessary result' of RTE's right to broadcast.
- There was no actual or potential substitute product available in the market to provide this programme information to the public.
- There was a keen demand by the public (potential viewers and listeners) for a seven-day advance guide listing all programmes, comprehensively, which RTE had failed to meet.
- There was no 'justification' for the refusal by RTE to supply the information even for reasonable royalties.

[42] At weekends for 48 hours.

In addition to these explicit grounds for a finding of 'exceptional circumstances' there is another implicit ground, the low-grade nature of the information contained in the programme schedules. This information came into existence not by act of individual creativity but as a necessary result of a commercial operation, which required for its success that this information be publicised widely and which, as highly ephemeral material, was of no further value or interest once the relevant programmes had been transmitted. The Court could not refer to this ground specifically because earlier cases had laid down a firm principle – that it is for the national Court to determine the scope of individual intellectual property rights – and both the UK and Irish Courts had held that such schedules are covered by the copyright law of those countries.

Nevertheless, the outcome of this case does illustrate the general trend in both courts and legislatures to draw the effective rights of the owners of 'informational copyright' more narrowly than of those with original cultural rights. Arguments raised by the parties under the provision of the Berne Convention limiting the situation in which compulsory licences could be ordered were not accepted by the Court. The remedy ordered by the Commission of compulsory licensing of the programme schedules was also confirmed. The European Court of Justice made, however, no comment on the method by which a reasonable royalty could be determined in such circumstances.[43]

Conclusions

This brief account of some of the changes which have been taking place in the treatment by legislative and judicial authorities of copyright, against the background of such fundamental technological and commercial advances, illustrates the pressures under which the owners of copyright (and indeed of all intellectual property rights) are now operating. In some respects reform of Intellectual Property Law has succeeded in clarifying and strengthening the rights of owners of copyright and their ability to exploit their rights on a world-wide basis. If the GATT arrangements affecting these rights are successfully implemented, this will be a major step forward. In other respects, however, especially as a result of recent EC developments and the *Magill* decision, such rights have clearly been limited both by the

[43] Such a decision in UK law could be rendered in the case of dispute under a collective licensing system by the Copyright Tribunal under Sections 116-143 of the 1988 Act.

emphasis of the European Court on 'exhaustion of rights' and also by the wide definition of 'abusive action' under Article 86 of the Treaty of Rome. The differing priorities held by the respective supporters of copyright and competition will continue to have to be reconciled on a pragmatic basis. What is clear in any case is the continuing need for inventive solutions to provide that reconciliation in both the short and the long term.

3

DIGITAL TECHNOLOGY IN MEDIA MARKETS: THE CONSUMERS' LIBERATOR?

Malcolm J. Matson

Chairman, National TeleCable Ltd.

Technology – Whose Servant?

NO INDUSTRIAL OR COMMERCIAL SECTOR IN THE WORLD boasts a richer vocabulary of technical jargon than does electronic communications – dominated by telecommunications, computing and television.

The multitude of telecoms, computing and television trade magazines or journals are littered with specialised technical terms, acronyms and alpha-numeric symbols denoting different aspects of high technology. In two of these arenas the old monopolies, British Telecom (BT) and the British Broadcasting Corporation (BBC), were responsible for pushing forward the technical boundaries of their respective sectors, and this has always been at the very heart of their corporate subconscious. Indeed, until relatively late in the day, these two public enterprises were, in concert with the dependent companies that exist as their equipment suppliers, the ultimate authorities on all aspects of their respective technologies – both present and future. Each set technical standards for its sector and dictated the limits of the use of emerging technology without risk of contradiction or competition. Predicated upon its own technical platform of 'today', BT and the BBC each mapped out a route to its own defined 'tomorrow'.

Within this self-defining technical environment, each perfected the subtle art of influencing public policy to ensure that it, and not the market, became the architect and time-keeper of the future – a future which, it could amply demonstrate, could only be reached from where it was starting. There was nothing devious or pernicious about this.

Each organisation had an unassailable confidence in its ability and obligation (laid upon it by government) to develop the 'right' technology at the 'right' time for the 'right' purpose.

A Horse-and-Buggy Parable

It is as if, late in the 19th century with the entire horse-and-buggy industry operating as a nationalised monopoly, an ingenious young blacksmith employed in one of the forges funded by this great state enterprise, invents the internal combustion engine. Senior management, delighted with this innovation, shares the good news with its ultimate masters – the government. The government considers what it should do to encourage and control the exploitation of this great technological advance for the benefit of the entire nation. Government officials busy themselves with consultants in 'understanding' the new technology and in seeking the advice of the blacksmith and his managers as to what should be done to further various interests. Officials bring forth an impressive Green Paper setting out a well-argued and fully quantified case for the specific costs and benefits to the horse-and-buggy industry, to travellers and indeed to King and country, if the internal combustion engine is 'properly' deployed.

Based on 'expert' advice, due weight is also given to the potential risks and not inconsiderable dangers that will be incurred – both to industry and to public – if this new invention is let loose on the world without the guiding hand of government, through regulation. It is argued that these new engines could malfunction in any number of ways with potential risk to individuals. Not only do they use a highly inflammable fuel but they are almost certainly lethal to anybody falling in their path. Thus they should only be driven by experienced vehicle operators – all of which are currently employed in the horse-and-buggy industry. Last but not least, too many of them appearing too quickly on the highways and byways would present an intolerable threat to both the physical and economic well-being of the large population of horses and the army of individuals involved in looking after, and otherwise supporting, them. Such devastating disruption to this large number of individuals, let alone to the nation's transportation system, must be avoided.

The public policy that eventually emerges in the form of a White Paper is widely applauded as being a 'good compromise' and in the best interests of all. It prescribes that the internal combustion engine will be licensed by the government for exclusive use by the horse-and-buggy industry throughout the UK in order to enable that industry to have, in advance of other countries, a standard means of transporting foodstuffs and other materials more quickly and economically to their own stables to feed the horses that are at the heart of their industry – 'always have been and always will be'!

So that nothing gets in the way of the full and rapid implementation of this ambitious plan, the government acknowledges that it will have to enact some minor 'enabling' legislation. The bill is soon published and with a healthy and vigorous debate in Parliament, finds its way on to the statute book – with only minor amendments – issuing no more than two licences for internal combustion engines in any one town (for at least seven years). A new regulatory body is to be established, to attach a technical approvals certificate to every engine, thereby certifying that it meets the agreed standards.

And true enough, the industry does become more efficient and the cost of transportation by horse and buggy does decline over the ensuing years. The blacksmith is appointed director general of ICE-AGE (Internal Combustion Engine Approvals and Guarantee Establishment). Progress is widely regarded as having been made. An enlightened UK government is seen to be working effectively in providing the statutory and regulatory environment by which the interests of both industry and consumers are promoted – helping to push forward the boundaries of technology to the benefit of both, whilst ensuring that their huge investment in horses is never threatened.

Vested Interests and Government Regulation

A parable maybe, but a situation very like it has prevailed until relatively recently in more or less every nation in the world in the electronic media industries of telecommunications and television. In some it still does. It was only rogue nations – notably the UK and USA – which started marching to another drum-beat in the early 1980s. Before that, a near-perfect global cartel of co-operating governments and collaborating operators persisted in many areas of the telecoms and television industry.

Superficially, such international unity of policy and technology deployment appeared essential in the communications industry above all others where, by definition, the transmitter and the receiver of information could be anywhere on earth but must, by definition, be able to 'communicate'. But just as in the parable, it restricted the market to exploiting technology of a form and in a time-scale which suited the cartel and not the user. ISDN (Integrated Services Digital Network) in the telecoms sector is a perfect example of this 'too-little-too-late' phenomenon which results from public policy that encourages the adoption of new technology in a manner and at a pace which ensures existing vested interests a place in tomorrow's world.

In more recent years, the UK government has properly adopted the stance that free-market competition, rather than government itself, is the proper engine for accelerating change and the appropriate arbiter of technological development. However, unwittingly and albeit for the very best of motives, the government still seeks to define its public policy and regulatory régime in the communications arena with explicit reference to specific current technology as deployed by vested interests and against *their* 'pre-defined' view of future developments in technology. In both the telecoms and the broadcast industries, governments tend to look and listen primarily to the vested interests of the industries themselves – the operators, advisors and equipment vendors.

Seldom, if ever, do policy-makers inquire whether the technical assumptions they are offered are either valid or indeed relevant. Indeed, who can they ask who is competent and truly independent and yet outside this closed system of vested interests? Certainly not consultants and probably not even all the academics – who feed the industry with students and are themselves fed by research grants and other helpful support. This highly incestuous environment results in the drafting of over-specific and detailed legislation and in a regulatory régime which makes unnecessary and unhelpful implicit, if not explicit, assumptions about present and future technology.

As a result, the tempo of change and deployment of new technology has, by and large, been slowed by the intervention of governments and the regulatory régimes they have created in the communications sector, to a pace which ensures the survival of existing vested interests by permitting them the luxury of unhurried and orderly adaptation. The infamous 'duopoly' policy of the 1980s in the UK telecoms sector is a good example. It was established 'in the national interest' so as to ensure that the two licensed operators were protected from competition to permit them time to adapt and cope with their changing environment. Such a government-sponsored slowing of the tempo of change is out of step with consumers' appetite for *any* perceived benefits which the new multi-media technology can bring.

The world enjoyed the unimaginable benefits of the internal combustion engine sooner rather than later because the horse-and-buggy industry was allowed to wither in a matter of years – thanks to the absence of government intervention and the imagination of users operating in a free market. It is all too tempting to use technology to achieve a smooth and orderly transition. That is precisely what vested interests wish to ensure. But it is the ability of technological innovation to do the very opposite – to make quick quantum or paradigm leaps – that makes it such a powerful tool for accelerating wealth creation, enhancing individual liberty and thereby improving standards of material and spiritual living. It can do so only if regulation lets the market be the prime arbiter of the deployment of new technology.

Britain's Unique Regulatory Environment

By happy accident, and as yet recognised by only a few, the UK now has a unique regulatory environment which has let the technological genie out of the bottle. When fully understood in the light of developments in digital and optical fibre technology, this new market will afford users and providers of information and communications services an awesome autonomy, giving them independence from the traditional vested interests of public telecommunications operators (PTOs) and terrestrial broadcasters.

The remainder of this paper describes, with the minimum of technical terminology, the defining elements of the technology of today's electronic media industries. It then outlines the paradigm shift brought about by developments in digital computing, optical fibre transmission and wire-less technology and concludes with an assessment of likely future developments in technology as deployed in the market.

The Technology of Communication in Telecoms and Television

Any act of communication implies that somebody wants to move something from one location to another – be it themselves, a letter, their voice, a moving picture, an iron girder, water, three tons of fresh fish, or simply information about a bank balance or the time of day. Although *information* (voice, video or data) is the specific focus of this paper, the basic principles which lie behind the choice of technology in any form of communication are best understood by appreciating the function of digital computing and optical fibre transmission technologies in the market development of electronic media communications.

Given certain 'content' is to be communicated between two parties, then three important factors bear on the decision how best to effect its transportation:

- the *quantity* to be moved (the quantum of each unit of that which is to be moved and the total amount of it to be transported);
- the *timing of its arrival* (by when must all of it have reached its destination?);
- whether each of the two parties is to *send and receive* (that is, does the communication require anything to be transported back to the sender?).

In any instance of communication, it is primarily the answer which the market provides to these three questions which dictates the choice of technology for effecting the transportation or communication. In a free market, the specific technology which will usually be developed or adopted is the one most cost-effective in moving all that has to be moved by the deadline by which it must all have arrived, to and from the designated destination(s). In other words, the varying requirements for *capacity*, *speed* and *two-way-flow* in a given communication determine the design and configuration of the medium used to effect that communication.

Two-way-flow is obviously essential to voice telephony. So telephone networks have been configured over the years with a topography that supports this capability. Mass market wire-less radio and television did not primarily emerge as industries requiring a capability for *two-way-flow*. However, the same principle of the inter-relationship between *capacity*, *speed* and *two-way-flow* applies to the wire-less communications of radio and television. There is nothing inherent in the technology itself which means that wire-less communications are different in this respect from wire-based communications.

Therefore, the first important principle to establish is that:

> *At given cost, varying requirements for capacity, speed and two-way-flow in any particular communication will be used by the market to determine the choice of technology for the delivery medium.*

There is nothing fundamental in the *technology* of radio and television (by wire-less or by wires) which necessitates either that they should be 'one-to-many' services or that the number of parties transmitting material is *de facto* limited by an absolute physical constraint relating to the *capacity* of the electro-magnetic spectrum.

The Electro-magnetic Spectrum and the Myth of Scarcity

This electro-magnetic spectrum can be described as follows:

High frequency	*Greater capacity* *Lower range and power*
cosmic rays gamma rays x-rays ultra-violet rays visible light infra-red rays radio waves electricity	
	Lesser capacity
Low frequency	*Higher range and power*

In general, the lower their frequency, the longer the range that the waves can travel and the less susceptible to interference from obstacles such as hills, buildings and rain. However, the information carrying *capacity* of waves increases as the frequency rises. Therefore, given that television started off in monopoly hands, with the consequential need to send the same signal throughout the land, an important trade-off had to be made. One extreme option would have been to build a single massively powerful transmitter at relatively low cost, to operate at low frequency in order to transmit the signal throughout the UK (and, as radio waves do not stop at the coastline, to much of Europe and beyond). At the other extreme, and at hugely higher cost, thousands and thousands of higher frequency but lower power transmitters could have been dotted around the country to provide much greater capacity but over a much smaller area. Originally there was no need for great capacity (only the BBC was in the market). Moreover, there were commercial, political and technological problems in building large numbers of high frequency transmitters and then linking them all to the single source of programming. Therefore, it is not surprising that the world ended up with a technical solution for its broadcasting industries towards the bottom end of the electro-magnetic spectrum.

However, recent developments in high frequency radio communications (such as cellular telephones) powerfully underline the point that for communications services that require high capacity (such as TV), the apparent scarcity of the spectrum diminishes as one moves up towards the higher frequencies. These frequencies have lower power and range and the identical frequency can therefore be re-used by other persons in adjacent areas. The lower the power, the nearer another person can be before re-using the same frequency without interference. Reduce the power so that the radio signal travels no more than a few yards between the antenna and the 'user' and the spectrum for the mass market suddenly becomes abundant – indeed infinite.

As regards wire-based technology, capacity has been radically transformed by developments in computing and optical fibre transmission technology (see Appendix, below, pp.78-82). Optical fibre transmission technology has several advantages, such as lightness, non-conductivity of electricity and the fact that digital formulae travelling down it scarcely fade, disappear or otherwise become lost or distorted beyond recognition (as when copper wires are used to carry analogue signals). However, the great prize this technology delivers is immense capacity because an optical fibre is physically capable of transmitting, simultaneously and in both directions, huge numbers of different binary formulae – all at the speed of light. To illustrate, one single fibre thread has the capacity (were its *full* frequency to be exploited) to carry over 1,000 times more than *all* the radio frequencies currently used for radio, television, microwave and satellite communications. Put another way, a single fibre thread has the capability to carry all the telephone traffic on British Telecom's network during the peak hour of the busiest day of the year. The telecommunications companies are not currently exploiting this immense capacity.

Carriage and Routeing

Given the requirements for capacity, speed and two-way-flow, two basic functions need to be performed to effect the communication. The first is *carriage* (moving the matter which is to be transported between the parties) and the second is *routeing* (directing what is to be moved from the originator to its destination). These twin functions of carriage and routeing are fundamental to all communication – not just electronic.

In the example of letter correspondence by Royal Mail, the postman and the mail train perform the *carriage*, and the various sorting offices along the journey perform the *routeing* – both in this case controlled and undertaken by the same entity, Royal Mail. However, if the letter is destined for New York, while the separate functions of carriage and routeing still persist throughout the letter's entire journey, they are no longer all undertaken by Royal Mail – US Mail is responsible for final routeing to the recipient's home. Similarly, a letter delivered across London by a cycle courier has its carriage and routeing performed by the same cyclist but the two functions remain distinct and discrete. The letter may fail to reach its destination because it is dropped *en route* or not even collected by the courier from the sender's office (no carriage) or it is collected but delivered to the wrong address (wrong routeing). The courier must successfully perform *both* functions to complete the communication.

In the case of a train journey, the engine pulling the coaches undertakes the carriage function and the signalman operating the signals and points performs the routeing function. In a car journey along a motorway, carriage and routeing are normally under the control of the car driver. However, under abnormal conditions (such as a serious accident), the motorway operator takes control of routeing and diverts traffic up a slip road. Nevertheless, as any car driver will know, the functions of carriage and routeing are truly distinct. Desperate to get to a meeting on time, you can be hurtling at 70mph the wrong way round the M25[1] for your destination (perfect carriage; bad routeing) or you can be stuck in a traffic jam *en route* for your destination (perfect routeing; poor carriage). In both cases, the communication fails.

The second important principle to establish is therefore that:

> *The functions of carriage and routeing are discrete. Each needs to be successfully completed before any communication itself succeeds. But there is no a priori reason why these separate functions must be undertaken by, or be under the control of, the same party.*

Developments in digital computing and optical fibres, described in the Appendix, have important implications for the functional segregation of carriage from routeing.

The Homogeneity of Electronic Information

First, all electronic information, whether originating as voice, video or data (sound, pictures or numbers), when in transit in a digital system, *is* now one and the same thing – a string of 1s and 0s. Any attempt to differentiate or categorise this particular formula of 1s and 0s from that particular formula of 1s and 0s, while they are passing down a strand of optical fibre or through the air in micro-wave form, is impossible.

1 London's circumferential motorway.

There is no longer any difference for, in transmission, video = data = voice. Any 'difference' is no more than an arbitrary imposition of a particular coding and decoding algorithm on the string of digits *before* and *after* they travel down the fibre or over the air. This coding and decoding function is controlled by the parties responsible for sending and receiving the information by means of computers under their *own* control and not by the network owner or operator. Although that party may also be undertaking the carriage function, it is not in its capacity as a carrier that it can exert any control over the content of what it carries.

The consequences of this for future regulation are immense. They suggest that any regulatory régime in telecommunications and television which is founded upon the premise that the *carrier* of the signal can and should be made responsible for the legitimacy of the content of the information will be fundamentally flawed.

By monitoring the flow of digits down a strand of optical fibre and nothing else (performing simply the carriage function), the network operator cannot know whether that stream of digits represents a human conversation, a Mozart symphony, an A4 page of FAX or drug money. The 'medium is definitely *not* the message': the owner of the transmission medium cannot be responsible for the algorithm which the sender adopts to code this or that particular information into a common commodity of binary digits.

This conclusion is important in the context of the debate about regulating the content of information on the Internet. Clearly, such regulation is not possible within the normal carriage function carried out by the telecoms network operator. However, there is every reason to expect that for political reasons, telephone companies will be slow to admit to their governments that they can no longer perform a 'content control or monitoring function' since, for reasons of national security, that was one of the main reasons they were originally taken into state control and ownership.

Patterns of Integration

Though technological developments have given many opportunities for the ownership boundaries of providers to change, the patterns of integration between the technical functions have, in practice, been far less subject to change. Take first the characteristic integration between carriage and routeing found nowadays.

Vertical integration between carriage and routeing can result either from the workings of a free market or from specific public policy and regulation. For example, the UK railway industry before 1992, had carriage and routeing undertaken on the railways by the same entity (British Rail). Today it is segregated between Rail Track which performs routeing and the various operating companies which undertake carriage. There is no *a priori* technical reason for arranging the railways one way or the other, though there may be political, economic or social reasons.

The conventional wisdom in telecommunications has been that these two critical functions of carriage and routeing are fundamentally integrated for reasons of technology. The concept of 'basic services' versus 'value added service' – so prevalent in telecom-talk of the 1980s – is founded on this very myth. Much of the world's current telecoms regulatory régime has falsely been founded on this assumption of necessary vertical integration.

Initially, in the very early days of telephony and broadcasting, entrepreneurial initiative in a free market gave rise to a high degree of vertical integration. Alexander Graham Bell laid the wires (carriage) *and* employed the telephone operator at the local exchange to undertake the routeing by switching and connecting those wires, although there was no reason why it *had* to be undertaken that way. He could have encouraged end-users themselves to get their 'own' wires to his central office where, for a fee, he would have performed just the routeing function by connecting one wire to another as and when required. However, it was the early intervention of government in the UK and elsewhere (in the name of national security) which caused this vertical integration to be established with the full force of law. Had governments not taken these industries to themselves at such an early stage in their development, competition might have emerged in the separate functions of carriage and routeing – just as it developed in merchant shipping which did not suffer monopoly government control.

In the 'wire-less' radio and television industries and also the cable-TV sector, as it has developed in the USA and is emerging in the UK, the *carriage* function is handled by the broadcaster or cable-TV operator itself (or its agent). Part of the *routeing* function is handled in the home by the viewer or listener: he or she turns the dial on the radio to a particular station, or presses a channel button on the TV set or cable set top box to select which of all the available signals reaching that receiver is directed to his loudspeaker or cathode ray tube. All the signals of every station and channel that *anyone* is capable of receiving in that particular geographic area (chosen by the operator of the carriage function to be made available) are carried right to the receiving equipment in the home over the airwaves or down the cable, and the consumer himself decides which will be *routed* over the final few centimetres of wire within that radio or television set to the loudspeaker or cathode ray tube. Therefore, freedom to route the 'right' signal to the end-user is actually in the hands of the end-user. However, even in this broadcast situation, where there is limited transmission capacity, the operator of the carriage function (the infrastructure operator) and not the end-consumer has the ultimate determination of what is available. If the broadcaster (whether by cable, satellite or terrestrial) does not 'carry' this or that programme in the first place, then there is nothing the end-user can do to 'route' it to himself.

So, unlike telephony, there was no integration of carriage and routeing to help sustain the argument that there should be a monopoly operator – simply that there was to be no two-way traffic which meant that government would itself be the sole originator of communications. The BBC and more recently, a restricted number of other franchised corporations, remain the only parties permitted to decide what material can be transmitted or communicated.

Out of this technical and historical background, two information delivery networks and infrastructures have developed to serve the mass market of end-users. Each has given rise to and is now supported by technologies configured as shown in Table 1.

Integration, Politics and Orderly Markets

So, contrary to conventional wisdom, it is the historical context of the development of these two industries and the politics of the day which have determined this outcome rather than anything inherent in the technologies. In the telecommunications industry, bundling the *carriage* and *routeing* functions together in the hands of a single operator has been a useful political tool to ensure, 'in the national interest', the preservation of a monopoly operator. Likewise, that the radio and television industries have ended up as one-way 'receive-only' media is not a function of some immutable law of physics or technology, but rather a consequence of political decision and/or oversight and the subsequent inertia of vested interests.

Governments across the globe have collaborated to ensure 'order' prevails at their national boundaries and have agreed a broadly common policy for the timetable and manner in which they will upgrade their outmoded networks with modern digital and optical fibre technology. This colossal replacement programme is timed to proceed

TABLE 1:
Configuration of the Television and Telephone Technologies

	TELEVISION NETWORK	TELEPHONE NETWORK
Supports high capacity/high speed traffic	Yes	No
Leaves routeing under 'end-user' control	Yes	No
Affords end-user freedom to transmit as well as receive	No	Yes

at a very slow pace due to the immense investment that is required to install the new technology and, because in most countries the telephone operator is still an agent of government, there are major fiscal and political implications to embarking on a swifter route to the future.

As a result, the developed world has telephone networks which, at the point where they connect to end-users, are constructed of low-capacity, out-of-date copper wires. This 'final mile' or 'local loop', as it is termed, was well able to support two-way voice telephony as intended by Mr Bell, but is severely restricted in terms of capacity and speed when it comes to bulkier signals such as video – despite certain advances in data compression. Likewise, there are the wire-less radio and television networks, based on an artificially restricted number of operators using high-powered transmitters covering very wide areas.

One of the main misleading assumptions behind public policy was (and remains) the belief that the *capacity* of the *ether* in terms of the number of radio or television stations that can be transmitted over any geographic area at one time is very limited and therefore the airwaves have to be carefully controlled by government to ensure the widest public benefit. 'Because it is so precious and scarce', it is claimed, 'it therefore warrants its allocation to the benefit of everyone being vested in the government rather than in the market.' While in one sense this is true, it is no *more* 'true' and tells us no more about how this capacity should be allocated than by stating, for example, that the total amount of real estate in the UK is 'finite' or the number of trees is strictly limited.

In a free democratic society, the apparent *ex deo* finite nature of any resource does not, of itself, justify denying individuals the freedom to own elements of it or to use their imagination in trying to make more out of their bit of that 'scarce resource' than someone else. Indeed, much more precious than scarce resources and much more to be conserved, is the freedom and opportunity to exploit them. Only when the opportunity for individuals to own and control any resource becomes seriously diminished as a result of a government-granted exclusive franchise, can the myth be perpetuated that in *this* instance, the 'scarcity' of *this* particular resource is fundamentally different and more serious than any other.

Once the policy was set with respect to the capacity required to transport wireless, television and radio signals, almost inevitably the resulting industry found itself in an entertainment cul-de-sac for most of its developing years. Entertainment (with a healthy seasoning of didactic news and documentary) was probably the only 'one-way' material that could be transmitted over the media and be seen as of direct benefit to the mass of the population which had been arbitrarily legislated into a passive 'receive only' mode.

But now the world is changing. The combination of digital technology and optical fibre has effectively placed the critical function of *routeing* under the software self-control of users of the network – whether consumers or service providers – taking it away from the hardware control of the network operator itself. The routeing directions of a telephone call (the numbers dialled on the originating telephone which define routeing and destination) become part of the communication itself and remain with that communication until it reaches its final destination.

Control by Users, not Operators

Digital telecommunication networks will increasingly behave like motorways rather than railways. The traffic itself and its drivers (end-users and service providers), which originate the digital formulae, will alone know the formulae and the destinations. Just like a motorway, and in stark contrast to a railway, a modern digital telecommunications network exists in an almost *passive* state as digital traffic routes itself to where it has been destined by the end-user, simply by 'looking at the signposts' on the network and routeing itself to its intended destination. This is in marked contrast to the highly active 'switching' function that had to be performed by the analogue network operator in order to route the traffic. In an all-digital fibre network, a network operator will never again have to answer the charge of having routed traffic to the 'wrong number'.

This technology-driven divestiture of control of routeing from network operator to network users has immense commercial and financial implications for traditional telecommunications operators (such as BT and Mercury) and also for the growing number of cable-TV network operators. Their core strategies are predicated on the assumption that, by making the huge investment in infrastructure, they can 'capture' the end-users' increasing expenditure on services – whether voice, video or data. Patently that is no longer true, as BT is beginning to discover.

When a telephone user in the UK picks up a telephone connected to the BT network and dials '1-3-2' to route his calls to the Mercury network and then dials the destination number, the only knowledge or measure that BT has of that particular call is its eventual 'absence' from the bottom line of its profit and loss statement. This powerful digital technology is being deployed in the UK in a regulatory environment that also promotes free competition in both the provision of services and the construction of networks.

There are therefore two separate and fundamentally different elements to the emerging 'information superhighway' and traditional major players (telecoms operators like BT and Mercury and broadcasters like the BBC) need to choose which is their core business. Is it real estate ownership (infrastructure provision) or retailing (service provision)? They are fundamentally different in all respects, just as, for example, investing in and managing the Commercial Union's property portfolio is nothing like running a McDonald's restaurant. Owning the infrastructure does nothing to guarantee success at retailing; vertically integrating the two simply increases the cost and risk of being in business in a free market. It may only be justified if the operator is sheltered from competition by holding some exclusive government franchise such that there is no market and the competition-free luxury of a monopoly annihilates any risk.

So, rather than investing in physical networks and local delivery infrastructure, given the technology shift, telecoms and cable-TV operators intent on selling telecoms and television *services* should be investing all their shareholders' funds *not* in building physical infrastructure but rather in a strong commercial relationship with a large consumer base and acquiring physical access to that customer base over the lowest-cost available delivery network – whoever owns it.

Seen in this way, the problem of 'interconnect' which, to the satisfaction of the vested interests, has for a decade diverted the telecoms industry and its regulator, is not an issue. The service retailers rather than the infrastructure owners will, by various voluntary contractual arrangements, negotiate access over any number of networks in order to reach their customers – just as they do when shipping physical goods around the world. This patchwork web of network infrastructures, each being in business for that very purpose (the carriage of third party signals and not their own), will be used by other competing service providers without fear of surrendering competitive advantage by using a network owned by its major competitor and yet gaining a substantial reduction in transmission costs.

The Threat to PTOs

Moreover, these developments in technology further threaten the very basis on which vertically integrated public telecommunications operators (PTOs) around the world currently derive their revenue. Almost without exception, the mass market around the world is charged for its telephone calls and most other communications on the basis of three factors:

- the time of day (if not week and year);
- the time duration of the call and the content – voice, video or data (the total number of 1s and 0s carried);
- the destination of the transmission (between caller and receiver).

That is to say, the user is charged a sum of money for each 'digit' transmitted and this sum varies depending on the distance between originator and receiver. Given that the capacity of a fibre optical cable in the context of the average mass-market user, can be regarded as *infinite*, and given that governments in the UK, USA and elsewhere are legislating to permit the development of competing networks, each of which comprises infinite capacity, simple economic analysis suggests that the market price will decline as more and more fibre capacity is deployed. The market price of digital transmission capacity is on a one-way trend – downward towards zero. Indeed, PTOs readily switch traffic remotely, many miles away from either caller or sender, even for local calls, now that the cost of transmission is so low compared to switching capacity. Nevertheless, the user is almost universally charged on the basis of the distance of the caller from the recipient rather than the total distance the 'digits are carried'. This is nonsensical – a local call can be made between two neighbours living 20 feet apart but, for whatever reason, switched 1,000 miles away and yet because it is a 'local' call, the end-user charge is a mere fraction of what the local phone company will charge to carry a call between two parties living, say, 40 miles apart.

Therefore, for PTOs to continue to derive revenues based upon charging a (high) price for each 1 and 0 users push down their infinitely capacious fibre networks, will require the concerted intervention of governments to reverse the declining trend of costs and transmission prices. Nothing less than such arbitrary control by government will maintain, even temporarily, a high price for a commodity in infinite supply.

Technology – Where Next?

What is now technically possible in creating, recording, communicating, manipulating and storing digital information, whether as sounds, pictures or a more complete 'virtual reality' may appear amazing. But this is only the beginning.

The technically *feasible* has never been and never will be a constraining factor in the media industries (nor is it elsewhere). For what the imagination of man can conceive, the ingenuity of engineers can realise. Without President Kennedy's commitment to put a man on the moon within a decade, it would never have happened, despite the latent technical genius of the Rockwell engineers. Technology has never, in isolation, shaped the future. It is only in a specific market environment that a technology rises to the surface to float *freely* between the eddies created by potential users and their demands or aspirations, on the one hand and, on the other, the commercial appetites of would-be suppliers – both vested interests and new entrepreneurial initiatives.

Public Policy Distortions

In the media industries of telecommunications and television there is an internationally forged and sustained overlay of public policy which seriously distorts the otherwise free emergence and adoption of new technology. In the early and mid-1980s, the UK deliberately broke ranks from this globally managed arena and, as a result of legislation then enacted, drew back from direct involvement in the development and promotion of specific technology. The lesson of ill-advised involvement in technology promotion – such as seen in the BSB satellite television débâcle – was a long time being learned and the cost was considerable. The Government's scepticism about European-wide initiatives, such as the Advanced Communications Technologies and Services programme (formerly known as RACE) or the Information Technologies programme (formerly known as ESPRIT), is even more justified. Like all such government-sponsored endeavours, they subsidise today's vested interests in manipulating the pace and form of change on a co-ordinated international front, to the disadvantage of consumers and market entrants.

Therefore, unless the British government decides to undo or tinker with its liberating legislation of the 1980s (which it will surely be urged to do by vested interests when it contemplates further primary legislation, especially under a new government), the United Kingdom probably presents the freest market in the world for the emergence and adoption of new technologies in developing multi-media markets. While the political climate in most countries is moving strongly in other directions, in Britain the Government has set itself firmly against any supply-side restrictions on telecom transmission capacity and will permit any party to lay as much fibre as it wants, wherever it wants. British consumers and service providers thus face the prospect – not available elsewhere – of limitless network capacity from a limitless number of providers. Therefore, the information super-highway (or rather, the information super-garden path) will emerge in this country ahead of the rest of the world.

Remaining Regulatory Obstacles in Britain

That is not to say the UK's current regulatory environment has no faults. Recently, radio has been used in voice and data telecommunications and a cable-TV industry is emerging. But neither development, given the manner in which it is taking place, will of itself yield consumers what they really want – freedom, wherever they are, to access a network with the following three 'star' characteristics:

- very high capacity;
- routeing under total end-user control;
- end-user freedom to transmit as well as receive.

Regulatory obstacles lie in the continuing artificial distinction between the carriage of telecoms and television signals which results in the responsibility for licensing these two activities being in different hands – respectively, the DTI and the Independent Television Commission (ITC). These two agencies appear to be pulling in totally opposite directions.

The DTI will grant any competent applicant a licence to construct and operate a network for the carriage of 1s and 0s to any home anywhere in the country – without regard to other licences granted to construct a similar network. In effect, this licensing régime is market-neutral. However, if those 1s and 0s represent broadcast television programmes, then another licence is required – granted by the ITC. The ITC has chosen (though it is not a statutory duty) to grant monopoly licences in any area of the country for the delivery of broadcast television over telecommunications networks. Clearly, this policy is not sustainable and the market would undoubtedly be further freed if government took steps to redress this anomaly – despite the inevitable cries that would be heard from US telephone company vested interests, now building cable-TV networks in the UK, that they would turn off the funding tap if the government so acted to remove their protection from competition.

Nevertheless, the UK remains probably the most attractive and fertile regulatory environment in the world for a market-driven adoption of new technology in mass media markets.

Specific Technology Trends in the Future

Future broad trends in technology and their implications for public policy include:

- Fibre technology has to date simply been deployed by vested PTO interests as a superior replacement for copper wires, coaxial cables, satellite links and micro-wave towers – connecting electronic computers (switches in central offices) to one another and with end-users. This computer technology will soon be seen for what it really is – an electronic bottleneck that results in only a minute fraction of the intrinsic capacity of fibre being used. An all-optical network or networks will eventually emerge which will result in the creation of a vast new error-free 'ether' – such that the electronic switching function currently undertaken within the network becomes redundant. There will no longer be a scarce capacity resource anywhere in the network which will require switches to allocate – the capacity of the all-fibre network will be so abundant that users can simulate any kind of logical switch. The exponential growth of the Internet is one of the first indicators of this.

- These all-optical networks will be increasingly passive and 'dumb' (just as is the air) and their ownership and management will increasingly equate to today's commercial real estate industry. They will be regarded as the 4th Utility. As the capacity of the all-optical networks will be infinite, users will no longer be charged on a 'bit-by-bit' basis (for each 1 and 0 transmitted). Ownership of these passive, dark-fibre networks will yield relatively low financial returns but will be regarded as extremely low-risk investments, providing highly attractive investment opportunities to institutional investors.

- The routeing function, traditionally at the core of the telephone companies' sources of revenue, will increasingly rest in the hands of users and service providers who will deploy computers and software under their *own* control to effect this. Just as the routeing function in the wire-less broadcast industry is performed by the end-user as he turns the dial of his radio receiver to route the station of his choice to his ears via the loudspeaker, so will users increasingly *route* the service of their choice out of the myriad that co-exist on the infinite web of fibre by 'tuning' into that service and 'routeing' it to the desktop, television screen or whatever equipment tomorrow will provide. The first glimpses of such a network, with the routeing function under the complete control of users, can be seen in the Internet which, when high bandwidth access to it from homes and businesses is available, will provide the 'virtual switching' referred to above – totally outside the control of the network infrastructure owner.

- In parallel with the organic (market-driven) spread of all-fibre open-access networks throughout the country, radio is increasingly likely to become the preferred medium by which end-users and their equipment interface with that network. The distance over which this radio connection is made will become shorter and shorter until, within each home, there will be various 'service specific' low-powered radio transmitters connecting the consumer's handset/terminal for that service to the single fibre network termination point – probably placed alongside the electricity and water meters. Homes will probably be built with the 4th Utility installed at the time of construction as it becomes regarded as just as essential as ensuring water and electricity are on-tap. This principle of user-radio control can already be seen in the cordless telephone or the cordless computer mouse. Choice and control of radio frequency will be up to the consumer and the manufacturer of the particular handset or terminal. Consequently there will be less room for government regulation as the market learns to develop its own method of allocating millions and millions of highly 'local' frequencies.

- Higher-powered radio will increasingly be reserved for the delivery of two-way mobile services and signals – whether voice, video or data. Eventually, consumers will have portable multi-media equipment capable of automatically switching frequencies (just as certain car radios do today) in order to gain radio access to the fibre network for the retrieval of the service/signal of their choice but via the antenna most appropriate to that individual user's position and other circumstances. In other words, more and more of the radio spectrum will be under the management and control of individual users rather than service providers – which will wish to get their service on to the low-cost and highly reliable fibre network as close as possible to the point of origination.

- More and more computer memory capacity will be dedicated to individual homes and be under the control of individual users and their equipment so they can store information (such as films and educational material), downloaded over the fibre network from remote data 'warehouses' for subsequent processing and consumption.

- The critical success variables for any would-be retailer of information services will be two-fold. *First*, access to a good product/service for which there is a demand. *Second*, access to a customer base from which it can collect payment for those services. Ownership and/or control of the infrastructure – all-optical or otherwise – will no longer provide any competitive advantages in terms of these twin success variables of service retailing. Indeed, it may be a positive disadvantage. From this one can conclude that the mega-mergers between network owners such as BT or AT&T, and product owners such as Murdoch or Ted Turner, will be short lived. The potential winners will be those who have invested in developing a strong relationship with a loyal customer base with which they transact commercial business.

- The digitisation of the world's information services will carry on apace and any meaningful distinction between television, computing and telecommunications will disappear. When a personal computer is available which can receive broadcast television and can make telephone and FAX calls, what is it? Who should regulate it? It is already possible to listen to real-time radio over the Internet or to make duplex[2] telephone calls, and yet what passes across the web of networks is nothing but 1s and 0s. Short of having a 'policeman' in every home to see how the digital stream deciphers, there is no longer any means of distinctly regulating voice, video or data – let alone distinguishing pornography from classical music.

- Digital compression will prove to be a valuable cost-reduction tool but *not* a primary technology for prolonging the life of low-capacity networks or removing the bottleneck caused by electronic switching.

Possible Consequences of the Technological Revolution

Just as with earlier industrial 'revolutions', there will be numerous unimagined consequences from this technological revolution – some beneficial, others apparently not. Technological change will continue to make many of today's concepts appear as 'peculiar' in retrospect as the idea that a man walking with a red flag should precede the horse-less carriage.

Consider, in the context of the technological developments outlined in this paper, the future rôle of what we now call the 'telephone company'. If I create (and own) the original analogue material (my end of the conversation), and these words are turned into digital code by a tiny low-cost computer (the digital-telephone) which I own and which is plugged into the fibre network serving my home for which I pay a modest monthly standing charge, and if I handle call-routeing by entering the right codes myself, what rôle is there for a traditional telephone company and what am I paying it for? PTOs as we know them are surely doomed, for if they survive on the basis of their current business, it will be little different from a government (or its licensee) arbitrarily interposing itself between the parties speaking in a face-to-face human conversation and then charging them both for the number of words spoken – factored by the distance they are standing apart.

---

2 Simultaneous two-way calls rather than A: transmit B: receive, then B: transmit A: receive.

Seen in this light, the owners of today's major media networks, such as the traditional telecommunications operators and the holders of broadcast television franchises, are increasingly becoming little more than government-sustained brokers who have, by means of their exclusive positions, managed to interpose themselves between provider and user of information and to extract an intermediary fee. Only in the absence of today's technology would there have been a legitimate rôle for such brokers.

Will the deployment of technology be controlled by today's brokers to prolong their existence, aided and abetted by naïve governments? *Or* will technology be deployed freely by the market, at the expense of today's vested interests? The latter is almost assured in the UK unless the government, now or in the future, mistakenly reverts to basing its policy on the 'expert' advice of those interests.

APPENDIX

Digital Computers and Optical Fibre Cables

The invention of the electronic *digital computer* at the end of the Second World War and its subsequent development and application alongside *fibre optic transmission* technology have revolutionised the world of electronic communications.

The Digital Computer

The everyday world presents itself to us via our sensory organs in *analogue form*, that is, as a continuous stream of apparently seamless sensation. Whether it is visual perception of the world, the sound of voices or music reaching us through our ears, or any other sensory perception of our existence over a period of time, what we perceive 'this' instant appears seamlessly and smoothly connected to what we perceived in the previous instant or indeed, what we will perceive in the 'next' instant.

Everyone is taught at an early age to understand that light and sound travel in smooth undulating waves. When he invented the telephone, Alexander Graham Bell created an 'analogue computer' which, when attached to both ends of a copper wire, could translate sound waves travelling through the air into electro-magnetic waves that could travel down the copper wire and then be translated by the second analogue computer back again into sound waves for the human ear to perceive – just as the original. The same underlying logical principle applies to television as we currently know it.

However, we also know that it is possible to re-create or represent accurately an apparently *identical* analogue sensation of seamless smoothness by stitching together individual snapshots or 'frozen slithers' which record phenomena at successive discrete moments over time. The earliest example of this that most people experience is the little book of cartoons which, when flicked through quickly, magically 'comes to life' with all the characters apparently exhibiting full motion. This *sampling* technique is used in the modern cinema. One of the main differences between the high quality of today's films and the jerky quality of a Charlie Chaplin film is the *frequency of the sampling*. A similar sampling approach is used in television, where the picture is broken up into small dots, called pixels, with average values of light intensity assigned for each pixel.

So the first way in which a digital representation of the world differs from analogue is in the *consideration of time*. In an analogue technology, time is continuously observed, whereas in a digital technology, time is sampled. However, this difference is more a matter of degree than of nature since a relationship between digital and analogue representations clearly exists if analogue technology is regarded as producing an *infinite number* of samples. This would imply that infinitely small amounts of time elapse between successive evaluations of the continuous variable. The digital notion follows directly from this idea by extending the time between successive samples. As the time between samples becomes large, however, the opportunity arises for the source signal or event to change without being observed.

An even more significant characteristic of modern digital technology arises from expressing these individual slithers of reality or time-samples in *binary numeric form.* By defining a code or devising an algorithm, it is possible to 'translate' each of these static slithers into a complex (and often very long) numeric formula.

To appreciate this at the simplest level, an analogue sound wave, plotted as a line on a graph with an *x* and *y* axis, can be expressed by a series of numeric formulae which define successive points on the curve in terms of *x* and *y*.

However, rather than express these numeric formulae in our everyday base 10 number system (0-9 notation) the individual *static slithers* of numeric values are expressed as *base-two values*, otherwise called *binary numbers*. A binary number is a number written in base two rather than our customary base 10 decimal system and therefore uses no other notation than 1s and 0s. Thus:

Decimal		*Binary*
1	=	1
2	=	10
3	=	11
4	=	100
105	=	1101001

The significance of using a binary numeric formula is that the '1' and the '0' can be represented by the 'on' and 'off' of a switch controlling the flow of an electrical current (however small) or a beam of light (a laser). Given that a silicon switch can change its state from 'on' to 'off' some 3 billion times a second, very long binary formulae can be created in a very small space of time and transmitted at the speed of light, faster than which nothing moves.

A *digital computer* is a machine with the capability of saving lists of these binary digital values and performing computations on such lists. Provided the computer is first given instructions (programmed) with the generally accepted rules on how to change information fed into it in one analogue form (for example, colour, number, sound, alphabet letters) into a binary formula, then the resulting string of '1s' and '0s' is the sole commodity it needs to process. For example, for letters of the alphabet, a simple standard code (ASCII) translates the letter P into the binary coding 0101 0000. Likewise, whenever the letter M is pressed on the computer keyboard, the binary string 0100 1101 is created inside the computer memory and is held there until it is instructed to do something with it.

An everyday instance of the use of digital technology is the compact disc (CD) which stores pre-recorded music. These silver plastic discs are devices for storing huge lists of formulae, all of which are made up of 1s and 0s. Each individual formula represents an individual time sample (static slither) of the original sound. When placed inside a CD player, the disc spins at a precisely controlled rate such that a laser built into the machine reads the lists of formulae (comprising just 1s and 0s) and 're-produces' the original analogue sound using precisely the same time interval between each slither or sample as was used in the original recording session. When amplified, the sound reaches our ears in waves from the loudspeaker, suggesting to us that we are present at the original recording session.

An obvious advantage of CD technology is the quality of the sound reproduction that it produces as a result of simply using the commodity of 1s and 0s. Because the only possibility of any error or distortion can be if a '1' is read as a '0' or vice versa, it is possible to use sophisticated methods to reduce the probability of this mis-sampling to virtually zero. There is no such thing as a fuzzy 1 or 0. This purity of information is implicit in all digital technology, which explains why the digital sound or picture is devoid of clicks, crackles and other blemishes common to the analogue world of reproduction. It also lies behind the truth of the familiar phrase in the computing world, 'garbage in – garbage out'. Hit a wrong key on the keyboard, thereby producing a formula with the 1s and 0s in the 'wrong' order for the purpose required, and that 'error' will be faithfully preserved and reproduced whenever that particular formula containing the 'wrong' information is stored, processed or otherwise used.

Fibre Optic Transmission Technology

Fibre optics is a branch of optics concerning the transmission of light by means of thin strands of glass or other optically transparent materials. Optical fibres can be used to guide light – which is electro-magnetic radiation in a certain frequency range – in much the same way that coaxial cables can be used to guide lower-frequency electro-magnetic radiation. An optical fibre is usually circular in cross-section and consists of a core and cladding. An optical fibre for communication applications is typically between about 0·1 and 0·2 mm (0·004 and 0·008 inches) in diameter.

Largely as a result of BT's pioneering work, Britain has been at the forefront of the development of this technology in telecommunications. In the modern telephone system, the principles of digital sampling and binary encoding outlined above, are used to convert a telephone voice conversation into formulae comprising 1s and 0s. Currently, this process of digital conversion takes place in the local telephone exchange, with the voice traffic having reached that computer in analogue form by travelling as electro-magnetic waves over two copper wires directly linking the exchange computer with the particular telephone handset being used for that conversation. Two individual copper wires connect every public telephone in the world directly to the telephone company's local computer switch. Eventually, this sampling and digital binary encoding of the telephone conversation will take place in the telephone handset itself but that will require users to re-equip themselves with digital handsets.

The computer at the telephone exchange can bundle the digital formulae from one particular telephone conversation with the formulae of other telephone conversations destined for the same local computer switch in some remote town or country. Bundled together using a different time-frame, these immensely long formulae comprising 1s and 0s – all of which have to reach the destination computer in 'real time' – are transmitted down optical fibre by a laser flashing on and off millions of times a second. The distant computer re-creates the original analogue sound from the binary formulae and delivers it as analogue sound down copper wires to the telephone handset of the party being called.

Just as sound can be sampled, so can pictures. Photographic imaging, whether by a television or a still camera, can now be done in digitised form, as when an A4 page of text and/or pictures is fed into a FAX machine. The images are scanned (sampled) to produce static slithers which are converted into long formulae comprising just '1s' and '0s' (about a quarter of a million for an A4 page). These then pass down the telephone wires as on/off pulses of electricity or pulses of light and are reconverted back into an image at the far end by reversing the scanning (sampling) process.

For television, the same principles apply but the length of the binary formulae become very large. In the UK, which uses the PAL system, there are 25 frames ('samples') per second. Each frame consists of pixels (see above) – 768 pixels wide by 576 pixels deep. In addition, there is the coding to define the colour of each pixel which in the UK is done on a 24-bit basis. A single frame of full motion TV uses 1·3 Mb of data or an hour requires the equivalent of nearly 450 CDs worth of raw data.

4

THE FUTURE OF PUBLIC SERVICE BROADCASTING

David Sawers
Writer and Consultant

BELIEF IN THE VIRTUES OF the 'public service' principle has been the basis of British policy towards broadcasting for the last 70 years: the state established a public body, the British Broadcasting Corporation, to provide radio and then television services, and provided it with finance through a hypothecated tax, the licence fee. Competitors financed by advertising have been allowed to enter the business in the last 40 years; more recently, satellite television services have appeared, financed by subscriptions as well as advertisements. But the competition has been strictly regulated – apart from that broadcast from space – and the BBC continues to be financed by the licence fee.

It has been the general belief of governments and the governing classes that only a tax-financed broadcasting organisation can provide high-quality programmes, and that the BBC and the licence fee should therefore be preserved. But the report of the Peacock Committee[1] in 1986 introduced into the debate a new element of concern and respect for consumers: it argued their interests would be best served by increasing the choice available to them, and by permitting them to influence what is supplied by encouraging direct payment for television services. The growth of commercial services, especially those distributed by satellite or cable and financed primarily by direct payments, has begun to implement the message of the Peacock Report. The media establishment has, however, counter-attacked to protect its traditional values, and the British government's policies now mainly reflect its views.

'Public service broadcasting' has often been defined as anything broadcast by a publicly-financed organisation, which is assumed to

[1] *Report of the Committee on Financing the BBC*, Cmnd.9824, London: HMSO, July 1986.

have the 'improvement' of its audience as its prime objective. It would be more logical, however, to define it as a service that provides programmes which are considered publicly desirable, but which might not be supplied by commercial services.

The main issues in the debate over the case for public service broadcasting are, *first*, whether the demands of the consumer should be the dominant factor in determining what services are supplied, or whether the state should intervene to ensure that programmes contain some other, 'improving' elements which consumers have not requested – and may not know they would like. The *second* related issue is whether in practice commercial services will fail to provide programmes which satisfy minority tastes, could be described as publicly desirable and promote the development of the arts and of popular taste for them.

Advocates of publicly-owned services, financed by taxation or licence fees, argue that commercial services will always give priority to maximising their audience, while publicly-financed services will seek to expand the audience's knowledge and understanding of the world. Those who put the consumer first maintain that commercial services will satisfy the demands of consumers if they are sufficiently numerous, while those financed by the state are liable to satisfy the demands of their producers rather than those of consumers. They may also be subject to governmental influence. The crucial question is, therefore, whether a competitive market for television and radio services can be established and maintained.

The Government has settled the immediate future of the BBC and public service broadcasting by proposing to renew its royal charter until the end of 2006. The BBC's sources of finance are, however, open to review at any time during the term of the new charter, and its dependence on the licence fee could be ended after 1 April 2002. The draft charter provides that the BBC could raise money from advertising, pay-per-view systems, subscriptions, or any other source of finance, if the Government and Parliament so decide. The Government therefore guarantees the BBC another five years of the licence fee, but leaves all options open for the longer term. These decisions therefore leave unanswered the fundamental questions: whether some form of tax-financed television and radio service is desirable when the number of commercially-run services is rapidly multiplying, and whether levying a tax to finance these services will remain politically acceptable once the number of alternative services has grown and the

BBC's audience has shrunk. This chapter will therefore review these questions.

Arguments for Public Service Broadcasting

The deeply-rooted belief throughout Europe in the desirability of publicly owned and financed broadcast services has been articulated more clearly as the number of commercial services has increased in the last decade. This belief is held most strongly among workers in the media, but also by many members of the intellectual élite and by politicians – not only those who favour socialist policies in other areas. It reflects the widespread suspicion of commerce and Americans among these groups; commerce and the profit motive are suspect, and commercial entertainment tends to be equated with Hollywood films and serials, which are said to weaken national culture. There is indeed a quite archaic emphasis on preserving national identities among many advocates of public service broadcasting.

These advocates feel that television is much too important to society to be provided on a profit-making basis. It is said, for example, to be for most people the main source of information about the world, of social concepts and of fantasies;[2] to supply a forum in which a nation can talk to itself,[3] and in which a society engages in the process of illuminating and either re-affirming, questioning or extending its existing values;[4] and which can offer a variety of ways of depicting social reality, so that the audience's curiosity is aroused and its thinking developed.[5]

Commercial broadcasting, which the system in the United States is held to exemplify, is believed to subvert quality and variety in programming to the objective of securing the maximum audience for the minimum cost. Competition is believed to intensify the pressure to achieve this objective, so that Professor Blumler has suggested that programme makers in a commercial system could be subjected to:

> 'rationalistic/calculative approaches to program planning and production; the frantic search for audience-maximising formulae;...the difficulty of

[2] Andrew Graham and Gavyn Davies, 'The Public Funding of Broadcasting', in T. Congdon *et al.*, *Paying for Broadcasting*, London: Routledge, 1992, p.181.

[3] Cited in J.G. Blumler (ed.), *Television and the Public Interest*, London: Sage, 1992, p.9.

[4] Graham and Davies, *op. cit.*, pp.186-87.

[5] Blumler and Hoffman-Riem, in Blumler (ed.), *op. cit.*, p.207.

> "knowing" one's audience, except through stereotypical images, when programs are destined for acceptance in multiple markets; factory systems of production...; and executive interference with program decisions in the uncertain pursuit of higher ratings'.[6]

He suggested that power would also be liable to shift from executives with programming experience to executives with financial or marketing backgrounds; and talented producers would then be less likely to work in television. A commercial system would therefore be expected to lower the standard of the programmes supplied to the public.

Commercial systems, it is also argued, are liable to provide news services distorted by the opinions of the systems' owners and the desire to satisfy advertisers. Only public service broadcasters are therefore able to provide unbiased, informative and authoritative news programmes. But eight out of 13 public service broadcasters are partially dependent on advertising for their income, so that few of them can claim independence of commercial influence.[7]

Possible solutions advocated by Professor Blumler and Dr Wolfgang Hoffman-Riem include procedures, in both commercial and publicly-owned broadcasters:

> 'To enhance the autonomy and rôle in organizational decisions of media professionals (for example, journalists) on the assumption that their norms will, on balance, accord more often with social and creative values than will the attitudes and incentives of media owners and managers.'[8]

Imperfections of Commercial TV Services

Economists have argued that the market for commercial television services will always contain imperfections, which can be rectified only by the provision of publicly-financed services. Andrew Graham and Gavyn Davies suggest there are three ways in which the market will fail to supply valuable external benefits to consumers:

---

[6] J.G.Blumler, *The Role of Public Policy in the New Television Marketplace*, Washington DC: Benton Foundation, 1989; quoted in Blumler (ed.), *op. cit.*, p.32.

[7] The five broadcasters that do not carry advertisements are the BBC in the UK, NHK in Japan, SVT in Sweden, ABC in Australia and the PBS in the USA. The PBS does accept donations and sponsorship from companies. (See *Public Service Broadcasting Around the World – A report for the BBC*, McKinsey and Co. Inc., April 1993.)

[8] J.G.Blumler and W.Hoffman-Riem, in Blumler (ed.), *op. cit.*, p.222.

1. It cannot ensure that programmes satisfy the preferences of those who do not watch them as well as those who do, although they should do so when programmes are believed to affect the way in which viewers will behave towards others – if they are believed to encourage violent behaviour, for example, everyone will be concerned about their content.
2. The market cannot work well when selling information: consumers do not know what they are buying until they have experienced it, and do not need to buy it once they have experienced it. The cost of a consumer's experiments with information should be no more than the marginal cost of supplying it; in the case of broadcasting it is zero, because adding one person to the audience for any one programme does not affect the other viewers.
3. Consumers are inevitably ill-informed about the effect that watching broadcasts will have on them, which includes the effect on their preferences for television programmes. Such effects will only become apparent to consumers in retrospect; so

> 'If all television is elicited by the market, there is a very real danger that consumers will under-invest in the development of their own tastes, their own experience and their own capacity to comprehend.'[9]

If consumers are to make the optimal investment in their own development, they therefore ought to be supplied with programmes of a higher quality than they would choose for themselves.

Graham and Davies also doubt whether commercial broadcasters would undertake as much research and development as is desirable, and whether they would not suffer from the deficiencies often attributed to British manufacturers – short-termism, reluctance to innovate, inadequate concern for quality and too little investment in training. They therefore consider the existence of a public service broadcaster in the BBC is essential for the health of the broadcasting industry.

Arguments for a Consumer-Driven System

The advocates of public service broadcasting attribute superhuman abilities to the producers of public broadcasting services: they are expected to provide programmes which make their viewers socially

[9] Graham and Davies, *op. cit.*, p.174.

more responsible, intellectually more demanding, and politically more inquisitive; and to entertain their audiences whilst inculcating these qualities. It seems implausible that such powers could be possessed by any group of human beings, however talented and high-minded; in practice their productions are bound to be influenced by their personal opinions and prejudices. The opposition to change in broadcasting – and to changing the BBC in particular – may well reflect the producers' fear that they will lose some of their freedom to produce what they like, rather than what the viewer wants or what the management thinks is affordable.

The description of what public broadcasting could provide is also difficult to reconcile with what the BBC actually supplies. These writings reflect a weakness in welfare economics, described many years ago by Sir Alan Peacock:

> '[Welfare economics] is a curious blend of often penetrating observation of the working of the market system with an astonishingly naïve view of the political and economic process.'[10]

A consumer-driven system has the advantage that it is known to work; it is what supplies consumer goods and services. Now that it has become technically possible for viewers to pay directly for the services they view, and for a multiplicity of services to be supplied – those subscribing to satellite or cable now receive about 30 television channels, which will increase five- or 10-fold soon with the introduction of digital 'compression' techniques – the market system has become equally suitable for broadcasting.

The first and most fundamental justification for this approach is that consumers are the best judges of what they want to watch. They will therefore gain the more satisfaction from their viewing, the more they can influence the selection of the programmes they see. The more choice of programmes they have, and the more they can influence the nature of the programmes offered to them, the more likely they are to find some programme they want to see. A wide choice of programmes also gives consumers more opportunities to develop their tastes by experiment, which is the most effective means of self-education.

Consumers can most effectively influence suppliers if they pay directly for the services they watch, so they can indicate the strength of

---

[10] Alan Peacock, *The Credibility of Liberal Economics*, 7th Wincott Memorial Lecture, IEA Occasional Paper No.50, London: Institute of Economic Affairs, 1977.

their interest in a programme by the amount they are prepared to pay for it, and support or disinterest are quickly translated into revenue gained or lost. This feedback from the viewer will operate most quickly and effectively if a pay-per-view system is used, but will still function, if more slowly, if payments are made for access to a channel. Suppliers will learn what the audience wants, and will alter the type of programme they provide accordingly.

A Paternalistic Approach

Attempts to supply something 'better' than the consumer would choose imply a paternalistic approach: the broadcaster knows better than the viewer what the viewer would like to see, and can provide programmes which will improve viewers by more than they would be improved by the programmes they would choose for themselves. Although the advocates of this approach believe it is a means of strengthening democracy by educating the electorate, there is inevitably the risk that it could degenerate into the 'big brother' approach of authoritarian régimes.

News programmes from public service broadcasters may be free from the influence of proprietors, but they cannot be entirely free from the influence of the politicians who determine the broadcaster's income. Public service broadcasters are therefore unlikely to challenge the political *status quo*. There is in any case little difference between public service and commercial news services in their dependence on advertising income: most public broadcasters get part of their income from advertisements, and most commercial news channels get much of their income from subscriptions. The influence of advertisers on the contents of new services is in any case often exaggerated: the newspapers of the Western world are not entirely prostituted.

A multiplicity of sources is the most effective guarantee that the public can receive unbiased information and comment on the news. With broadcasting as with the press, freedom of entry and controls over ownership will protect the public interest more effectively than can the provision of a publicly-owned news service.

The benefits of experimentation in the development of consumers' tastes make choice desirable in itself. The more choices consumers have, the better they can develop their tastes. Policy should therefore seek to weaken barriers to entering the television business, so that the number of services can be maximised. The 'free' services provided by public service broadcasters are bound to be fewer in number than those supplied commercially, because the limits on tax revenue will limit the number of services that can be supplied.

The supposed advantage to consumers of being able to try services at no immediate cost cannot improve consumers' welfare if it reduces their choice of services. The existence of tax-financed services, which are free at the point of consumption, is bound to reduce the demand for commercial services – especially those which are financed by direct payment. It will also affect the character of the commercial services provided: demand will be strongest for services which are different from those available free. Competition between tax-financed and commercial services will tend to reduce the diversity of the commercial services provided.

Direct payment for services can improve, rather than reduce, the welfare of consumers if it increases their ability to secure the supply of the services they wish to see. Under public service broadcasting, consumers may be able to try services at no cost, but they can only try those services that the producers think they ought to see. These producers may be influenced by the audience figures or other market research on the viewers' desires, but they have less incentive to meet these desires than the managers of a commercial service, which has to satisfy viewers to earn a living. The public service system of establishing consumers' desires by market research is that used so unsuccessfully to plan the production of consumers' goods in the Soviet Union.

The paradox that consumers cannot tell how much they would want some information or service until they have received it, and no longer need to pay once they have experienced it, applies to all forms of entertainment. But such ignorance is not absolute. Anyone planning to see a play or hear a concert cannot know precisely how he or she will react until it has been experienced: but they, like television viewers, may have seen or heard other works by the same artists and may have read about their other performances. The same work may well be performed more than once, so that word-of-mouth reports on it can be transmitted, or reviews read. The process of choice is a continuous one, not a series of independent events. The more opportunities consumers have to test out their tastes, the more they can develop them; and the number of alternative services will be limited if they are financed by taxation. Variety and choice will be maximised if services are provided on a commercial basis, and consumers are free to decide how much they will spend and what they will spend it on.

Advocates of public service broadcasting adopt a naïve and self-contradictory approach, desiring independence from political interference, but finance from taxation: complete political independence is not consistent with dependence on government for money. Commercial services, financed by a variety of means, are more appropriate to a democratic society.

The Evolution of Policy

The Government announced its decision to maintain the *status quo* in a White Paper published in July 1994,[11] after eight years of discussion that had followed the publication of the Peacock Committee's report in July 1986.[12] The Government's commitment to reform of the broadcasting system in general – and of the method by which the BBC is financed in particular – gradually weakened during this period, and showed the influence of the arguments for public service broadcasting outlined above. The Peacock Committee had recommended that

> 'The fundamental aim of broadcasting policy should in our view be to enlarge both the freedom of choice of the consumer and the opportunities available to programme makers to offer alternative wares to the public'.[13]

The Committee therefore proposed that the BBC should, in the longer term, move from reliance on the licence fee to reliance on subscriptions as its main source of finance. This view was endorsed, as a long-term objective, in the Government's White Paper on broadcasting in 1988, which stated that

> 'The government looks forward to the eventual replacement of the licence fee. The timing will depend on experience gained ... of BBC and other new subscription services'.[14]

By the time the Government had published a consultation paper on the future of the BBC in November 1992,[15] the continuation of the licence fee was clearly the favoured option, and the conclusions of the 1988 White Paper were ignored. It was not therefore surprising that the White Paper of 1994 should propose that the royal charter of the BBC should be renewed for 10 years when it expires at the end of 1996, although it also proposed that the system of finance through the licence

---

[11] *The Future of the BBC*, Cm.2621, London: HMSO, July 1994.

[12] Cmnd.9824, *op. cit.*

[13] Cmnd.9824, *op. cit.*, para.547.

[14] *Broadcasting in the '90s: Competition, Choice and Quality*, Cm.517, London: HMSO, November 1988.

[15] *The Future of the BBC*, Cm.2098, London: HMSO, November 1992.

fee could be altered after 2001. When the draft of the new charter was published in November 1995, the date for such a change had become any time after 1 April 2002.

The 1994 White Paper is a notably vacuous document, which essentially states that the BBC should carry on as before, providing programmes that cater for all tastes, whilst also supporting the arts and reflecting the national identity – but broadcasting less bad language, sex or violence, and more about science, engineering and industry. The main innovation is the proposal that the BBC should try harder to exploit its assets commercially, by selling its services to commercial broadcasters or co-operating with them.

The use of subscriptions to finance the BBC is described as impracticable in the immediate future, only becoming possible when most people can receive digital transmissions. In fact, subscription would be possible with the existing analogue transmission system, as shown by the Government's own published studies and the operations of Canal Plus in France, although it might become simpler to introduce with digital terrestrial transmission systems. The Government proposed[16] in 1995 that the BBC should broadcast its existing services on digital channels without charge, but left open the possibility that the BBC, like other companies, could use digital channels for additional services (see Chapters 3 and 5).

The new charter[17] provides the legal basis for changing the sources of the BBC's funding by including the provision that the BBC can raise money from any commercial source – advertising, sponsorship, subscriptions or pay-per-view – if the government approves this action. It would therefore be possible for the BBC to use commercial sources to finance any of the additional digital services it could provide.

The 1994 White Paper concludes that 'in the longer term' it may be possible to transfer all or some of the BBC's service to a subscription service, although it also criticises subscription, and the encryption of services it entails, for ending universal access to BBC programmes.

The Government has thus postponed decisions about the financing of the BBC until the next decade, when other Ministers will have to face up to the case for change. The technological possibilities will be clearer by then, and the BBC may have begun to use commercial sources of

[16] *Digital Terrestrial Broadcasting. The Government's Proposals*, Cm.2946, London: HMSO, August 1995.

[17] See Cm.517, *op. cit.*, and Cm.2098, *op. cit.*

finance for some additions to its basic services. But its commercial rivals are likely to have gained in strength at its expense: the proportion of homes receiving cable or satellite services is generally predicted to have increased from 21 per cent at the end of 1995 to around 50 per cent by 2000, so that the BBC's share can be expected to fall.

Willingness to pay the licence fee will inevitably decline with the BBC's share of the audience; and opposition to the fee is likely to grow more than in proportion to the decline in the audience, because the people who subscribe to cable and satellite services will be richer than those who now object to paying the fee, who – to judge from prosecutions and surveys – are mostly those with low incomes, women and single parents. Future objectors are likely to be more articulate and politically more influential.

Attitudes to the Licence Fee

It is not clear whether the licence fee is now considered acceptable by the majority of viewers at its 1995 level of £86·50, which has remained stable in real terms since 1988. Survey evidence is contradictory, with much greater dissatisfaction expressed in surveys which invite people to express their opinions about a range of public services than in those which ask for their opinions about broadcasting services alone. Such differences are apparently a common feature of market research surveys. Table 1 shows that 62 per cent of those interviewed in the National Consumer Council's Consumer Concerns survey in 1990 thought the price charged for a television licence was unreasonable and only 25 per cent thought it reasonable. The percentage unhappy with the licence fee increased as incomes fell, so that 74 per cent of those with household incomes of less than £6,500 thought the licence fee unreasonable.[18] Earlier NCC surveys produced very similar results.

However, only 25 per cent of those questioned for the BBC in 1993 thought the licence fee was poor value and 64 per cent thought it good value, although 64 per cent were also opposed to any increase. This survey also found that only 32 per cent of respondents thought the licence fee was the best way of financing the BBC, while 31 per cent thought a combination of licence fee and advertising would be the best system.[19]

---

[18] *Consumer Concerns 1990*, London: National Consumer Council, August 1990.

[19] *BBC's Response to the Consultation Paper on the Future of the BBC*, Opinion Survey by Research International, May 1993.

TABLE 1:
Satisfaction with the Licence Fee (per cent)

Licence Fee Considered	NCC 1990	BBC 1993
Very reasonable/very good value	3	24
Fairly reasonable/fairly good value	22	40
Neither	9	9
Fairly unreasonable/fairly poor value	23	15
Very unreasonable/very poor value	39	10
Don't know	4	1

Sources: *Consumer Concerns 1990*, National Consumer Council;
BBC Response to the consultation paper on The Future of the BBC, 1993.

Support for the belief that existing television services (whether the BBC's or advertising-financed commercial companies') are not popular is also provided by the NCC's survey. It found that 52 per cent of respondents were dissatisfied with the quality of television programmes, and only 32 per cent were satisfied. But the BBC again found its respondents were happier with the *status quo*; 76 per cent were satisfied with BBC1 and 61 per cent were satisfied with BBC2.

The high level of video recorder ownership in the UK – about 75 per cent[20] in 1994 – and the expenditure by their owners on recordings to watch on these machines, which is about 80 per cent of their spending on the licence fee[21] – also suggests many viewers are dissatisfied with the BBC and ITV services. Satellite and cable services have built up their penetration to 21 per cent of homes within little more than six years, despite high subscription charges; and most forecasts suggest that this share will rise to about 50 per cent by 2000. It therefore seems reasonable to believe that many people are dissatisfied with the television programmes they now receive, and that there is an unsatisfied demand in the UK for a wider choice of television programmes.

Creating a Competitive Market

The retention of public service broadcasting would be desirable only if a competitive market for television services could not be created and

[20] *Family Spending: A Report on the 1994-95 Family Expenditure Survey*, Central Statistical Office, London: HMSO, 1995.

[21] *Screen Digest*, March 1995.

maintained. If a truly competitive market existed, in which consumers could exert their influence on suppliers, there would be no obvious need for public service broadcasting. Consumers could decide how much to spend on television programmes, just as they decide what to spend on other services, and the licence fee could be eliminated. Such a market is technologically possible; whether it is established depends on government policy as well as the presence of entrepreneurs. Effective policies to preserve freedom of entry are required, but they will not be easy to implement.

The crucial technology for a competitive market is that which allows the broadcaster to collect subscriptions from viewers by 'scrambling' the television signal and collecting payments from viewers who are supplied with the means to 'unscramble' the signal. There are strong incentives to have only one system in each market, because viewers do not want to pay for two units to unscramble the signal in their homes. Whichever company is first to establish a subscription system is therefore likely to establish a monopoly, and can use its position to control the terms on which newcomers can enter the market. In the existing analogue TV services, British Sky Broadcasting (BSkyB) operates the dominant system in the UK, while the French company Canal Plus owns the dominant system on the Continent.

The introduction of digital services, with a vast increase in the number of channels available and the need for new technology, will provide the opportunity to introduce more competition to the market. The European Community therefore introduced a directive[22] to try to maintain competition in October 1995, and the British government published its proposals[23] for implementing this directive in January 1996. They seek to ensure that all broadcasters can use a system on similar terms, so that its operator cannot determine the conditions on which other companies can enter the market.

In an ideal world, a subscription system would be operated by a third party, which did not provide television services. In practice, a subscription system for digital services is likely to be operated by a dominant company like BSkyB, unless a group of broadcasters forms a consortium to operate a system. The regulators will therefore have a difficult task, because the operator will always have an advantage over

[22] Directive 95/47/EC of the European Parliament and the Council of 24 October 1995, *Official Journal of the European Communities*, 23 November 1995.

[23] *The Regulation of Conditional Access Services for Digital Television*, Department of Trade and Industry, London, January 1995.

the potential users of its system. The British government proposes that the Office of Telecommunications (OFTEL), which regulates competition in the telecommunications industry, should also regulate the digital television services; it will issue licences to operators, which must not discriminate unduly among broadcasters, must offer fair and reasonable terms, must keep separate accounts for their subscription service, and must supply OFTEL with any information it requires.

Operators are not required to publish the terms on which they will provide their services: the Government proposes that this should be a penalty for misbehaviour. Publicity is, however, the most effective protection against misuse of market power; so a requirement that suppliers of subscription services should publish a tariff of charges would be a very desirable addition to the Government's proposals.

The biggest barrier to entry in the British television industry, however, is the licence fee. The existence of an organisation financed by a tax on all television viewers, which controls more than 40 per cent of the market, must be a powerful deterrent to potential new entrants. The fact that many companies have recently entered the market is, of course, an indication that the BBC is considered vulnerable to competition, and that many viewers are dissatisfied with the service it provides. But there would almost certainly have been more newcomers, offering a wider range of programmes, if the BBC had not possessed so advantageous a financial position.

Experience in the USA has shown that competition from the free services of the Public Broadcasting System (PBS) has hampered the development of commercial services providing cultural programmes: out of four networks established in the early 1980s to provide cultural programmes, only one has survived – the Arts and Entertainment channel, formed by a merger between the Arts channel and the Entertainment channel. The three difficulties these services faced were that the potential audience was small, the costs of original programmes were high, and the Public Broadcasting System was already providing cultural programmes in 40 per cent of its broadcasting time – at no direct cost to the viewer. It was also spending heavily on these programmes: indeed, its expenditure is greater than that of BBC1.

David Waterman concluded, after a study of this experience, that the commercial channels had faced a hopeless task in trying to compete with the PBS for this small audience: they could not afford to match its spending on programmes, and could not get enough viewers to pay their subscriptions when the PBS was offering very similar services without charge. The same situation would apply in Europe, he suggested, though the potential audience might be larger.[24]

The strength of a public service broadcasting network can therefore be an obstacle to the development of a wide range of commercial services. Until the public broadcasting service is switched to commercial funding, it is impossible to judge whether there are any gaps in the services provided which might justify government intervention. The parallel with the press would be for the government to finance a broadsheet paper by a tax levied on all readers of newspapers, and make it available free to the public.It is unlikely there would be as many serious newspapers on the market as there are today, if they were faced by such competition.

Is There a Case for Subsidy?

The case for any government intervention to finance television programmes after a competitive market is established depends not only on the existence of gaps in the types of service provided, but on those gaps being in services which provide social benefits worth more than the cost of subsidising their supply. It is not just a matter of saying that commercial services would not provide 'enough' cultural programmes, for example; it has to be shown that the social benefits of providing more cultural programmes exceed the cost to the taxpayer of supplying them.

It is not at all obvious that the social benefits from cultural programmes *additional to those for which viewers are willing to pay* would justify any subsidy. The arguments used to justify subsidies to the arts are not convincing: the widespread belief that the arts cannot be flourishing and innovative unless they are subsidised is not supported by the historical evidence, which shows that the arts did flourish in the centuries before subsidies were first provided in the 1940s. The arguments about external economic benefits from the arts to society are similarly weak. The most plausible case is that they can benefit education, and that education in the arts can improve an individual's welfare.[25]

---

[24] David Waterman, 'Arts and Cultural Programming on Cable Television: Economic Analysis of the US Experience', in N.K. Grant *et al.* (eds), *Economic Efficiency in the Performing Arts*, ACE, University of Akron, 1987.

[25] See David Sawers, *Should the Taxpayer Support the Arts?*, Current Controversies No.10, London: Institute of Economic Affairs, 1993.

There does not therefore seem to be an argument for state subsidies for cultural programmes, although there may be a case for supporting educational programmes. Children are a special case, in that they do not possess the purchasing power to support their desires, and may not be aware of the benefits they will receive from education. They may fail, therefore, to demand the types of television programme which will help the development of their tastes, so that they can appreciate the arts better in adult life; and they are more likely to fail to demand the straightforward educational programmes which may be linked to school courses. Children depend on their parents to purchase such services for them. But parents may be unaware of the benefits their children can gain from education – or educational television – and so be unwilling to pay for it. Moreover, they may not appreciate that children, even more than adults, will benefit from exercising the power to choose what they watch.

The state therefore has a rôle in supporting education, deriving from its duties to children and a desire to see them educated to be responsible and useful citizens. This rôle may be considered to extend to supporting television programmes which help the education and development of children. It is, however, a long step from stating this principle to defining the programmes that might be supplied to meet these objectives. The most appropriate body to determine how much public money should be spent, and what sort of programmes should be supported, would be the Department of Education.

Any support for programmes would depend on the Department of Education judging that the programmes supplied by commercial broadcasters were inadequate for the development of children's knowledge and attitudes. Such programmes could be produced by independent producers or by any of the several specialist children's channels, and broadcast preferably on any channel that was not encrypted – such as the ITV network – as well as any children's channel that wished to carry them.

The Future of the BBC

If there is no justification for public service broadcasting and so none for the licence fee, the BBC will have to find a new rôle. The Government's decision to extend its royal charter until the end of 2006 postpones this necessary change. Sir Alan Peacock has said that his committee envisaged the BBC would be largely subscription-financed before the end of this century,[26] but the Government's desire to avoid decisions means that the conversion of the BBC's main British services to subscription will not have begun by that date.

The BBC is an institution that has dominated British cultural life for the last 70 years, has one of the finest news services in the broadcasting industry, and has recruited enough creative talent to be able to provide a first-class entertainment service as well. But it has recently seen its income cease to grow, because the conversion from black and white to colour television sets has ended and the licence fee has been linked to the retail price index. It is also an organisation that has been characterised by a previous head of BBC news and current affairs, Ian Hargreaves, as having 'hideous management problems', which are

> 'endemic in an institution like the BBC, which is a paradigm of inefficiency: it has, essentially, a single paymaster, which implies a centralised process of fund allocation and answerability, but the BBC has simultaneously constructed a honeycomb of operational units or empires to foster creative independence. ...The fact that this structure is prodigiously wasteful was not controversial so long as the BBC was a monopoly or near-monopoly supplier. ...It is the change in the competitive environment which has precipitated the BBC's current managerial crisis. ...A creative enterprise as large and structurally rigid as the BBC, run without market discipline, will naturally tend either to be under insufficient managerial and financial control, or to be so checked by managerial system and restraints that its creative edge is blunted'.[27]

Drastic changes in the BBC are therefore needed, and the only means to eliminate the weaknesses Ian Hargreaves identifies would be to transform it from a producer to a publisher of programmes, with the drastic reduction in staff that this entails.[28]

The present emphasis on stricter and more centralised controls over expenditure can be expected to drive out some of the BBC's creative staff and therefore to reduce its creative output. It has been criticised for its harmful effects on the quality of television drama by Andrew

---

[26] 'Minutes of Evidence Taken before the National Heritage Committee', House of Commons, *The Future of the BBC*, 25 May 1993, London: HMSO, December 1993.

[27] Ian Hargreaves, *Sharper Vision*, London: Demos, 1993, pp.30-31.

[28] Adopting the publishing format has allowed a number of the new ITV contractors to reduce their costs compared with their predecessors.

Davis, himself a successful television playwright, who argued for delegating decisions on what was broadcast to producers.[29]

Continuation of present policies implies that the BBC's share of the market will continue to decline, because the quality of its output will deteriorate and creative staff will depart. This development is desirable: creative work can be done more efficiently in small organisations, so that such moves by BBC staff would improve the performance of the British television industry. The value of the BBC lies in the abilities of its staff; the public will gain if these people are freed to work in more favourable surroundings, rather than held inside the BBC.

But these internal changes would not help the BBC to fit better into a competitive, commercial market-place. A decline in its market share would make it less of a barrier to entrants; but as long as it receives the licence fee, it will possess a competitive advantage over other broadcasters which have to earn their income from the viewer. The solution proposed by the Peacock Committee was that the BBC should switch to subscriptions as its main source of income. But the objective should be to transform the BBC into one of many commercial broadcasters, with complete freedom to determine how it earns its income in a competitive market.

Cut the Licence Fee

Government policy should therefore be to start reducing the BBC's dependence on the licence fee as soon as the new Charter permits, in 2002. It should then allow the BBC to make up for the loss of revenue by employing the power granted in this charter to raise money from any commercial source it chooses to exploit.

The 1994 White Paper said the BBC should not have to rely on advertising for its income because it would affect the character of its programmes, and that other broadcasters – the ITV contractors – feared that their income and that of the press would be reduced if the BBC took advertising. The claim that advertising would force the BBC to become populist is implausible; the BBC frequently boasts of the large audiences its programmes obtain, and clearly believes it needs to attract large audiences to justify its receipt of the licence fee. If advertising is one part of an organisation's income, and many other companies are advertising in the same market, advertising is less likely to influence programming and advertisers are more likely to be seeking minority audiences.

---

[29] Andrew Davis, *The Huw Weldon Memorial Lecture 1994*, televised on BBC2, 2 January 1995.

Concern for other advertisers is probably exaggerated, and certainly misguided. It is exaggerated because advertising revenue can be expected to increase at a rather faster rate than the growth of the economy. Moreover, analysts[30] now seem agreed that an increase in the supply of advertising time will increase total advertising expenditure – the Peacock Committee was advised that it would lead to a reduction, which strengthened the arguments against using advertising to finance the BBC. The concern is misguided because no firm has a guaranteed right to any source of income. In a market economy, any firm is free to seek to exploit any market, and there is no reason why advertising-financed television services should be sheltered from competition. Advertisers and consumers could be expected to benefit from greater competition. If the BBC wants to enter the television advertising market, the firms now living off this market will have to become more efficient.

Once the BBC's charter has expired at the end of 2006, it should be sold; the licence fee payers, who have financed it, and its employees would be the most appropriate shareholders for the privatised BBC.[31] Its ultimate rôle should be as a privately owned, commercially financed broadcasting organisation.

The transition to purely commercial sources of finance would not be easy. If the BBC chose to make all of its services available only to subscribers, it would have at some point to take the unpopular decision to encrypt the services – and so bar them from those who did not pay. It might well consider that some of its services should remain freely available; in a digital world where it could have more than two channels, one possible course would be to limit encryption to additional services. The more expensive programmes might then be available only on subscription. Open access to encryption systems, as will be required, implies that viewers already subscribing to other digital services should be able to use their existing equipment to subscribe to the BBC.

To move from a BBC funded by the licence fee to a BBC that earned its income commercially would take at least five years, to give the organisation time to build up its commercial income. The licence fee

---

30 See 'Minutes of Evidence Taken before the National Heritage Committee', House of Commons, 24 June 1993, Annex II to Evidence of Robin Foster, 'The Television Advertising Market', in *The Future of the BBC, op.cit.*

31 Ways in which ownership of the BBC could be given to its customers and employees are discussed in detail by Jeffrey Gates in an appendix to Ian Hargreaves, *op. cit.*

might be run down gradually during this transitional period. The size of the BBC thereafter would depend on its commercial success. Commercial pressures could be expected to complete its transformation from a producing to a publishing organisation, because the need to improve efficiency would then be greater.

BBC co-operation with commercial channels should be strictly controlled, whether or not it is funded by the licence fee. The licence payers would benefit if the BBC earned more by selling its programmes to other broadcasters, if the proceeds were used to reduce the licence fee or to improve services; but they would not benefit if such transactions, or co-operative agreements, increased the market power of other large companies. As the largest organisation in the British broadcasting industry, the BBC's market power should not be increased by collaboration with other companies, nor should it be used to increase the market power of large private sector companies. Such increases in market power would magnify obstacles to entry and so reduce the choice of services available to viewers. The BBC should therefore be included in the Government's controls over concentration in the media business.

The Problem of Radio

Radio services cannot be financed in the same ways as television, because it is not practicable to encrypt and charge for radio programmes: the cost of the encryption system would be too large in relation to the cost of a radio set or the revenues that could be obtained. Advertising and sponsorship are therefore the only practicable commercial sources of income. They could be supplemented, however, by voluntary subscriptions and donations. They provide nearly half the income of the public broadcasting systems in the USA – about $800 million a year[32] – and there is no reason why these sources of funds should not be tapped by British broadcasters as well.

The public appears much more satisfied with the quality of radio programmes than it is with television; the National Consumer Council found that 68 per cent of respondents to its survey in 1990 were satisfied with the quality of radio programmes, and only 6 per cent were dissatisfied. The BBC was the largest supplier of radio programmes in 1990, so this response suggests that its radio services were better liked than its television services.

---

[32] *Statistical Abstract of the USA, 1994*, Table 894.

The Peacock Committee recommended that Radio 1 and Radio 2 should be financed by advertising; but this advice was not accepted. It suggested that other BBC radio services should continue to be financed by the licence fee. Radio accounts for about 25 per cent of the BBC's expenditure; a radio-only licence fee would be about £25 for 1995 (about £20 if Radio 1 and Radio 2 were excluded) if the cost of collection was the same as for the television licence. If the licence fee was retained to finance all radio services when it was abolished for television, radio listeners would be left with a significant charge. A radio-only licence fee might prove more difficult to collect than a television licence, because fewer people listen to BBC radio than watch BBC television. Fifty-nine per cent will listen to BBC radio some time in a week, while 92 per cent will watch BBC television.[33] But the BBC had a larger share of the radio than the television audience at the end of 1994 at 48·6 per cent,[34] compared with 44 per cent for television.[35] The BBC's share of the radio audience is likely to fall, because more commercial stations started operating in 1995.

The figures in Table 2 show how little correlation there is between the audience for each service and its cost. Radio 5's audience may be expected to increase as it becomes more familiar – it started broadcasting in its present form in March 1994 – so that Radio 3 is the odd man out: its cost is 76 per cent of that of Radio 4, but it has a tenth of the audience. It also has less than half the audience of Classic FM, its closest commercial rival, which has shown there is a demand for classical music that the BBC had failed to exploit. Radio 3 is the most obvious candidate for finance by voluntary subscriptions. Its small audience limits the amount of advertising revenue that could be earned, but its audience includes a core of regular listeners who should be prepared to contribute to the cost of the service. If Radio 3 could not be financed by subscriptions from listeners and companies which may benefit from its existence, and any sources of commercial revenue, there is little reason for the taxpayer to intervene. If the service is considered to have educational value, the Department of Education might subsidise it; but Classic FM, which appears to have enlarged the audience for classical music, might be thought equally deserving of support. Services like Radio 4 and Radio 5 would also be suitable for a

[33] BARB/RAJAR figures for 1994.

[34] See Table 2.

[35] BARB figure.

TABLE 2:
BBC Radio Audiences and Costs: Fourth Quarter 1994

	Radio 1	Radio 2	Radio 3	Radio 4	Radio 5	Local	All
Reach[1] (per cent)	23	19	5	18	10	21	59
Market Share[2] (per cent)	11·3	12·8	1	10·6	2·7	10·2	48·6
Cost (1994-95) (£ million)	£32·8	£37·5	£56·0	£74·0	£34·7	£118·4	£353·4

[1] Reach = percentage of population listening for at least 15 minutes in each week.

[2] Market share = percentage of total hours of listening devoted to each channel.

Cost of local radio includes £45m cost of regional services.

Sources: RAJAR figures, quoted in: *Key Note, Broadcasting in the UK*, 1995 Market Report; and *BBC Annual Report and Accounts 1994-95*.

combination of commercial and subscription finance, although their larger audiences would make commercial sources more feasible. More popular services like Radio 1 and Radio 2 could be financed mainly by advertising; although the Radio Authority has suggested that only Radio 1 could be profitable if financed by advertising alone, costs and services can both be changed, while advertising revenue and rates can be expected to go on rising.

Local radio services are one category that might merit some public sector support, but this aid should come from local authorities, not central government. If any local authority believed that a BBC local radio station performed a useful function in its district, it should be free to support it out of locally collected taxes. To judge from American experience, local stations would also be likely beneficiaries of subscriptions and donations from individuals and businesses.

As with television, however, it should be for the BBC to decide how its services should be financed, once it had been given commercial freedom and the licence fee was on its way out. Its commercial freedom also implies that it should be free to change its radio services as it wishes, and not feel bound to preserve services which it now provides. The pattern of radio as well as television services is likely to be changed by digital technology. Commercial freedom would provide the best environment in which to exploit the new technology.

Conclusions

Public service broadcasting is an idea that has had its day. When the number of services that could be broadcast was limited to a few by technology, and consumers could not pay directly for the services they used, there was some sense in providing a tax-financed television service that tried to be universal and impartial. Now the number of services that can be provided is limited by demand rather than technology, and consumers can pay directly for what they use, there is no value in this idea – if the principles of a liberal economy and a democratic society are accepted. Consumers now have the ability to make their demands known to suppliers, and to choose between suppliers. They should be given the freedom to use these powers.

The only defence for public service broadcasting is that defects in the market prevent consumers exercising their power effectively. Consumers do not have perfect knowledge in this market, but such imperfections are not unusual – they apply to other forms of information and entertainment. These imperfections do not imply that a tax-financed supply of choices, selected by the producers of a state-run television service, is better than the choices offered by the market in response to the demands of consumers. The market is likely to supply more choices than a state-run system, and it will be more responsive to the wishes of consumers. The market is not perfect, but it is better than an imposed service.

Those who still believe that a tax-financed public broadcasting service is better than a commercial service, financed by its users, hold an essentially paternalistic view of society. They assume that consumers cannot know their own best interests, but that television producers can. This attitude attributes implausible abilities to television professionals and is inconsistent with democratic governance: it implies that an intellectual élite should be able to choose what the public sees and hears, and should determine how their opinions are developed. Such power is dangerous.

If the principles of liberal democracy are accepted, consumers should be able to obtain what they want, not what somebody else thinks they should have. They are most likely to do so if the choice of programmes available to them can be maximised. The objective of policy towards television should therefore be to increase the choice of programmes available to the consumer.

This objective can best be achieved by maintaining freedom of entry to the television business, which implies that both commercial organisations and the BBC should be prevented from achieving dominant positions. It implies also that the Government should strengthen the proposed regulation of subscription services, and extend its controls over concentration in the media to include the BBC.

Government's main task should therefore be the maintenance of competition. It is encouraging that the Government is showing more interest in regulating concentration in the broadcasting industry, because competition is the key to ensuring the consumer benefits from its development. While the BBC still enjoys the benefits of the licence fee, it is particularly important that it should not be allowed to use the commercial strength this income provides to create alliances which establish lasting market power.

It is a long way from the Government's present policies to those which would be economically and socially desirable. It is also a long time before major changes in the financing of the BBC can be made. In the interval between now and 2002, government should consider when it wishes to see the licence fee terminated, and when it should start to run down the licence fee to reach this target. Growing public resistance to paying the licence fee will be one factor it will have to consider in judging how long it can be retained. The Government may well find that pressure to end the BBC's dependence on the licence fee has become irresistible by the time the new charter permits a change in the BBC's sources of finance in April 2002.

The sooner the BBC knows when the licence fee will end and what the timetable may be for its run-down, the easier is the transition likely to be. A review of the BBC's sources of finance should therefore start long before 2002. The change from a state-owned organisation financed by its private tax to a private sector company competing for viewers' payments will be difficult, and it should be given plenty of time to plan and to implement it. A new board of governors will also be needed to oversee the change. The sooner they are in post, the better.

Necessary decisions about the future of the BBC have only been postponed. The longer they are delayed, the more difficult they will be and the more likely it is that they will be forced on government by increasing resistance to paying the licence fee. If half the viewers are subscribing to cable and satellite services, will they willingly pay the licence fee? How many people can the BBC prosecute for non-payment in a year? And what will happen to the electoral support of a government that tries to maintain the licence fee against strong opposition? These are some of the considerations which should make politicians act soon to replace the BBC's licence fee, and to create a consumer's market for television services.

5

A POLICY FRAMEWORK FOR THE MEDIA INDUSTRIES

William B. Shew
Visiting Scholar, American Enterprise Institute

Irwin M. Stelzer
Director of Regulatory Policy Studies, American Enterprise Institute

Introduction

DEVELOPING A POLICY FRAMEWORK FOR THE MEDIA INDUSTRIES means balancing two conflicting considerations. On the one hand, government should not preserve or create boundaries between industries that technology is causing to converge. Given technology's rapid advance, this consideration speaks for a minimal government rôle in the media industries. On the other hand, government cannot ignore the media's special rôle in a democratic society: if the distribution of information becomes concentrated in too few hands, the diversity of news and views so essential to an informed populace could be imperilled. Policy-makers should avoid creating a regulatory strait-jacket that impedes the development of economically optimal business organisations, while remaining sensitive to the need to preserve competition and diversity.

It is now widely accepted that 'convergence' is blurring the lines between computers, communications, consumer electronics, publishing and entertainment.[1] Like many technological revolutions, this one creates difficult policy questions: Should British Telecom be allowed to

[1] See, for example, Department of Trade and Industry, *Creating the Superhighway of the Future: Developing Broadband Communications in the UK*, London: HMSO, November 1994, p.4. Chapter 3 of this *Readings* discusses recent and prospective technological developments.

offer video-on-demand, including the programming? On what terms should cable companies be given access to telephone networks? How much media cross-ownership should be allowed? How can regulatory policy encourage, or at least not discourage, the optimal development of new technologies?

The principles that can guide one through this maze of problems seem clear: allow consumer choice to drive decisions, and avoid inhibiting the flow of resources in response to those choices. In addition, prevent an accretion of economic power that would deny consumers access to a wide variety of services and opinions. The complexity involved in putting these principles into practice is illustrated by one of the principal issues now confronting policy-makers: cross-media ownership. That policy debate is complicated by the rapid evolution of media technology and by three myths: that the media industry is highly concentrated; that media cross-ownership is unnecessary to the industry's development; and that existing regulations place some media companies at a competitive disadvantage and thereby distort competition.

To develop a rational regulatory policy, it is necessary to dispose of these misconceptions and to consider the subtleties demanded of policy-makers in a transition period, lest government be led to tinker in a counter-productive manner with a regulatory régime that is far more progressive than in most countries. As the DTI points out in reviewing policies affecting the 'information superhighway', the success of Britain's policy of 'progressive liberalisation and the encouragement of new entrants has been remarkable: prices have fallen as services have been improved and widened'.[2]

The media industry is in a period of transition that will reduce scarcity and widen consumer choice. Terrestrial channels now dominate television in Britain. Unlike satellite and cable TV, which currently serve fewer than one in four homes because of their cost and (in the case of cable) limited availability, terrestrial channels are universally available. But their number is limited, giving those who control them substantial economic and 'cultural' power.

This power is constrained by competition from other media – newspapers, magazines, radio – and by the new television delivery systems, satellite and cable. But it remains significant enough to warrant close scrutiny. The need for such scrutiny stems from the huge

---

[2] *Ibid.*, p.1.

market share enjoyed by the limited number of terrestrial channels – four or perhaps five, in the immediate future. When digitalisation and compression permit a multiplication of terrestrial channels – to perhaps 20 or 30 – policy problems will ease. Meanwhile, policy-makers have to respond to the existing situation *without* impeding the desirable development and introduction of technology that will eventually permit a considerable expansion of the number of terrestrial channels. In short, they must be sufficiently subtle to deal with a technological revolution by protecting the public *now* without damaging its long-run interests.

Media Concentration and Diversity

Concerns about media power are far from new. At the turn of the century, when the media consisted principally of newspapers, the power of press barons was decried here and abroad. When electronic media and cinema emerged, the caricature of the press baron was replaced by that of the media tycoon.

Large media enterprises have traditionally attracted two broad concerns. The more conventional is the general one – economic power. A highly concentrated media industry might be able to charge consumers and advertisers prices significantly above competitive levels. The second concern attaches to the media's rôle in disseminating information. In democracies, the belief is widely shared that the political and cultural health of a society is fostered by numerous, independent media, competing vigorously and providing a diversity of views. The media operate as gatekeepers, mediating between consumers of information and potential suppliers. If the gatekeeping function is highly concentrated, the public's access to important information or viewpoints could be harmfully restricted and independent voices could find it difficult to gain access to a wide audience.

The danger posed by media concentration is sometimes characterised as a loss of diversity. But the connection is not clear cut. In a highly concentrated market, a few firms account for most of the output. Diversity, on the other hand, may refer either to the number of independent media companies, regardless of how small they are (diversity of sources), or to the variety of viewpoints expressed in the media (diversity of content). Thus, a media industry that is unconcentrated may nevertheless exhibit little content diversity – thousands of media voices each saying much the same thing and attracting similar audiences. And a media market that is concentrated may nevertheless exhibit great diversity – independent voices of every possible political stripe and cultural view, with a few capturing most of the public's attention.

There is little to suggest that UK media lack diversity of views. Kiosks overflow with upwards of 600 newspapers and nearly 8,000 magazines and periodicals, counting only those published domestically, representing every imaginable interest and point of view. More than 40 television channels are now available to the viewing public, ranging from general interest channels to all-news formats, landscaping and country music channels. Radio is flourishing, with over 150 local radio stations and four new national networks in addition to the five operated by the BBC. Cinema, rebounding from a decline in the 1970s, has more than 2,000 screens across the UK.[3]

But is the UK media market concentrated? In their competition for the public's attention, some media products are inevitably more successful than others. Early in 1996 the most popular daily national newspaper sold more than 14 times as many copies as the least popular.[4] Top-selling magazines boast circulations 10 to 15 times as large as the typical magazine. BBC 1 attracts a national audience three times as large as Channel 4's, and 50 times that of a typical satellite or cable channel.[5]

Moreover, many corporations have multiple media holdings. Some companies specialise in a particular media segment. Others, in pursuit of media synergies, are attracted to cross-media ownership. The BBC, in addition to its terrestrial television and radio activities, has become a significant magazine publisher and supplier of satellite channels. Newspapers have branched out into satellite television, radio, and the cable industry. Thus, the availability of a broad range of media

---

[3] Unless otherwise noted, all circulation data for national newspapers are from the Audit Bureau of Circulations; data for regional and local newspapers are from the Newspaper Society; data for magazines and periodicals are from *British Rate and Data*; data for television are from the Financial Times's *New Media Markets*; data for radio are from Radio Joint Audience Research Ltd. and the Association of Independent Radio Companies; and data for the cinema are from the Financial Times's *Screen Finance*.

[4] *The Sun* had a circulation of 4,128,485 in January 1996, as compared with 292,049 for *The Independent*.

[5] In the week of 18 February 1996, for example, BBC 1 attracted a national viewing share of 33·3 per cent, as compared to 11 per cent for Channel 4 and a combined total of 9 per cent for over 40 satellite and cable channels. (*Source*: *New Media Markets*, Vol. 15, No. 8, 29 February 1996, p.12.)

products, as characterised by subject matter and viewpoint, does not preclude some concentration. If some compete far more successfully than others for the public's attention, then – despite diversity – some concentration may occur.

Whether concentration co-existing with media diversity constitutes a problem, let alone one soluble by public intervention, is disputed. It is one thing if media concentration is the consequence of restrictions preventing the entry of new media players, and quite another if it is the outcome of consumer choice in a free and open media market. But even when concentration is the outcome of some companies' superior ability to satisfy the tastes of the public, a concern is sometimes expressed that those companies might wield excessive influence as a consequence. But is the UK media industry currently concentrated? That is the question to which we now turn.

Measuring Concentration and Diversity

How to measure concentration depends on one's purpose. We consider, first, the more traditional matter of economic power. We then turn to whether market structure might restrict or unduly concentrate the flow of information.

Economic Power

Media industry classifications are designed more for statistical convenience than for measuring the extent of competition. The relative shares that media organisations have of these classifications, therefore, often have little meaning. An economically meaningful market is one in which producers compete for customers – which is often much wider than the market for physically similar products. To say, for example, that a firm 'controls' 100 per cent of the white handkerchiefs produced in Britain does not necessarily mean that it can influence price unilaterally. There is competition from imports, from existing producers of substitute products (coloured handkerchiefs, tissues) and from potential entrants.

In television, terrestrial broadcasters have their own trade association and use a technology different from other purveyors of entertainment, news and information. But they do not compete simply among themselves. Terrestrial broadcasters increasingly face competition for audiences and advertising from cable and satellite television, radio and the print media. A discussion of media competition cannot be framed in terms of traditional industry classifications alone; it must include an analysis of competition across the entire media industry.

Intermedia Competition

Newspapers, magazines, radio and television all compete for the consumer's attention. The intensity of competition depends on the degree to which consumers regard different media products as substitutes. Clearly, 'quality' newspapers[6] such as *The Times* and *The Telegraph* vie with one another for readers. Less obvious, but also important, is the competition between newspapers and magazines for customers' patronage and time. Witness the tendency of Saturday and Sunday newspapers to add extra sections to win readers not only from each other but also from magazines. Fashion sections in newspapers compete with fashion magazines; book review sections compete with literary magazines; television listings in newspapers substitute for magazines devoted to publishing listings.

Intermedia competition for the public's attention does not stop with rivalry among print products. The print media, television, radio and other electronic delivery systems all compete with one another. Evening news programmes on television have had a profound effect on the demand for, and character of, evening newspapers. The marked shift of regional and local newspapers from evening to morning editions is widely attributed to the growing competition from evening news broadcasts on TV and radio. And the increasing use of colour in daily newspapers, like the increased use of sophisticated graphics in print media, is a direct result of readers becoming accustomed to such attention-getting devices on their television screens. The massive investment by newspapers in new colour printing, a phenomenon not confined to Great Britain, is designed to increase the attractiveness of their products relative to other media, as well as other newspapers.

These competitive battles are reflected in the ebb and flow of audience ratings of radio stations and TV channels and the circulation of newspapers and magazines. But in addition to the cyclical give and take of competition, long-term trends in intermedia competition can be discerned. None is more striking than the seemingly inexorable success of the electronic media in luring audiences away from the print media, particularly newspapers. Between 1986 and 1992, average daily circulation of national 'quality' newspapers in the UK declined by

[6] 'Quality' newspapers are typically broadsheets, as distinguished from a tabloid format.

almost 300,000. According to a statistical analysis[7] we performed to identify the sources of newspaper circulation trends, almost a third of the decline is attributable to the steady expansion of TV services over the period.[8]

The media segments also compete with one another for advertising. That competition is closely related to the competition for audiences, of course, since advertisers buy access to audiences. National newspapers compete for display advertising with television and the four new national radio franchises, and to a lesser extent with local radio. Local radio competes more closely with the local and regional press than with television and national newspapers. But media-buyers constantly monitor developments in advertising rates – the cost per thousand readers or viewers implied by a company's advertising rate card – with an eye to reshuffling advertising funds to achieve the most effective exposure at the lowest price.

This competition has led to a marked shift over time in the shares of advertising expenditure captured by the different media. As new technologies have been introduced and expanded, they have cut significantly into the share of advertising revenue going to more traditional media. A striking example is television, whose share of advertising expenditures between 1954 and 1994 grew from zero to 32 per cent. Radio has also come to occupy a more significant rôle, increasing its share from just over one-half of 1 per cent in 1954 to nearly 3 per cent in 1994, its highest percentage to date. Meanwhile, the share of advertising expenditures going to national newspapers dropped slightly, from 17 to 15 per cent. The share for regional newspapers fell more substantially, from 31 to 21 per cent, as did the share for magazines, which fell from 32 to 15 per cent.[9]

---

[7] One of us (Shew) has performed several analyses of the demand for newspapers, in terms of both the aggregate sales of newspaper segments (for example, daily tabloids, quality Sundays) and the demand for individual newspaper titles. The circulation of a newspaper (or newspaper segment) is related statistically to its (average) cover price, the prices of competing newspapers, promotional budgets of newspapers, *per capita* personal income, availability of TV channels, and so forth, using monthly data from 1986 through 1992. (See William B. Shew, 'Determinants of Newspaper Circulation' (mimeo), March 1994.)

[8] The supply of TV services has expanded in several ways: the number of TV channels has increased, the typical broadcast day has been lengthened, and cable and satellite TV have become more widely available.

[9] The Advertising Association, *Advertising Statistics Yearbook 1995*, Oxfordshire: NTC Publications Ltd., 1995, pp.29-33.

The extensive intermedia competition for audience and for advertisers should not obscure the fact that the most direct competition is often found within the individual media segments.

Intramedia Competition: Newspapers and Magazines

More than 600 newspapers are published in Britain, producing sales of more than 140 million copies every week. Including the 700 free sheets – which compete vigorously for advertising and provide increasing amounts of editorial material – nearly 175 million copies circulate weekly.

At present the UK has:

- 11 national and 90 regional paid-for daily newspapers;
- nine national and 12 regional Sunday newspapers;
- more than 500 paid-for and nearly 800 free weekly regional newspapers; and
- approximately 7,800 magazine and periodical titles.

Not all these publications are close substitutes. Equally, it would be wrong to argue that regional papers do not compete with national titles, or that free sheets do not compete with paid-circulation newspapers for advertising business. Strong regional newspapers, owned by financially powerful chains, are becoming such a competitive force (in part, by combining to offer advertisers national coverage) that the national newspapers are being forced to develop regional editions. Both types of newspapers compete vigorously with magazines and other print products for readers and advertisers.

The degree of substitution between any two newspapers (or newspaper segments) can be quantified by measuring the circulation gain achieved by one when the price of the other rises by a small amount. The substitution pattern revealed by econometric analysis is consistent with intuition: competition is more intense within conventionally defined newspaper segments than between segments.[10] When a national tabloid increases its cover price, the other national tabloids experience sharper circulation gains than do national quality

[10] William B. Shew, 'Determinants of Newspaper Circulation' (mimeo), March 1994.

newspapers or regional papers. Readers seem particularly ready to substitute one tabloid for another.[11]

But readers of the quality press are also quite responsive to price changes. *The Times*'s daily circulation has soared by 334,000 (more than 90 per cent) since its initial price cut in September 1993. Some of that gain represents a net expansion in total newspaper sales. But the remainder of *The Times*'s gain seems to have been from a broad range of newspapers: other quality dailies (mostly *The Telegraph*, far less *The Guardian* and *The Independent*), quality Sundays, the tabloids, and, not insignificantly, regional papers.

An important additional feature of newspaper competition is the high degree of supply substitutability. If a publication attempts to impose onerous conditions on advertisers, or pay less attention to product quality, it quickly finds not only that advertisers and readers switch products, but also that competing producers offer new products very quickly.

The most important factor for media regulators to consider, however, is the marked decline in barriers to entering newspaper publishing. Changes in printing technology, less restrictive labour practices and improved distribution systems have all worked to lower publishing costs and make small-scale entry more feasible. In 1977, the Royal Commission on the Press grimly reported that the newspaper industry was in poor health. Papers were failing, and the unions had a stranglehold on the industry. The Royal Commission found that four of the eight national dailies and six of the seven Sunday national newspapers were making losses. It concluded: 'the financial position of the industry is poor and … is becoming critical'. Newspaper proprietors such as Roy Thomson and Cecil King agreed, predicting that only five national newspapers would survive in the UK. All that is changed. Costs have been reduced and barriers to entry lowered. Since 1981, nine new national newspaper titles have been launched. Four have survived and now account for a tenth of national newspaper circulation.[12]

---

[11] The greater reluctance to switch from one quality paper to another may reflect their greater product differentiation and less sensitivity to price among their readers, who tend to have higher incomes.

[12] *The Mail on Sunday* (1982), *The Independent* (1986), *Sunday Sport* (1986) and *Independent on Sunday* (1988) are still in circulation. *Sunday Today* (1986), *News on Sunday* (1987), *The Post* (1988) and *The Sunday Correspondent* (1989) have not succeeded; nor has *Today* (1986), which ceased publication in November 1995. Other new launches have included *Scotland on*

TABLE 1:
Average Weekly Television Viewing,
Week Ending 18 February 1996

	Hours	Viewing Share	
		All Channels per cent	Ad-Supported per cent
BBC	12·06	43·7	0·0
ITV	10·04	36·3	65·5
Channel 4	3·03	11·0	19·8
Cable/Satellite	2·30	9·0	14·6*
Total	27·43	100·0	100·0**

• About 90% of cable and satellite viewer hours carry advertising.
** Numbers do not sum to 100% due to rounding.
Source of column 1: *New Media Markets*, Vol. 14, No. 8, 29 February 1996, p.12.

Intramedia Competition: Electronic Media

The electronic media are characterised by less competition than the print media. That is especially evident in television, where the dominance of terrestrial TV is reflected in viewership data. The four terrestrial channels, BBC1, BBC2, ITV and Channel 4, account for over 90 per cent of all viewing (see Table 1). The share of the two BBC channels is over 40 per cent, while Channel 3 attracts almost 40 per cent. Channel 4 attracts only 11 per cent, while all satellite and cable channels account for only 9 per cent of viewing hours.

The dominance of terrestrial television is explained in important part by its less expensive technology for distributing television signals. Non-terrestrial transmission requires substantially larger investments: satellite transponders, uplinks, and reception dishes for satellite TV, or a costly landline distribution system for cable TV. As a result, the average household must pay about £20 per month to obtain access to cable or satellite transmissions, unlike terrestrial TV, which is essentially free.[13] Not surprisingly, only 23 per cent of households are connected to a cable-TV system or have a satellite dish.

Sunday, *Wales on Sunday*, *Daily Sport* and unsuccessful attempts to resuscitate two London evening newspapers, *Evening News* (1987) and *London Daily News* (1987).

[13] The BBC licence fee is not a deterrent to watching the BBC since it is payable by all homes with television receivers. According to the Cable Communications Association, most operators charge around £15 per month for basic cable service (in addition to a nominal installation fee),

For advertisers, TV concentration is even greater than these figures suggest, since the BBC and some cable and satellite channels carry no advertising. When programming not carrying advertising is excluded, ITV obtains a nearly two-thirds share of viewer hours (Table 1, final column). Channel 4 obtains just under 20 per cent, and cable and satellite channels account for less than 15 per cent. ITV presents the only practical option for an advertiser wishing to reach a large national television audience.

Radio broadcasting, which not so long ago was characterised by even less competition than television, now appears quite competitive. In addition to the BBC's five national radio services and roughly 40 regional and local services, private-sector operators now provide four national services and over 150 local services. Private radio, supported by advertising, has proved highly successful in competing with the BBC. The BBC, whose domestic radio monopoly was not legally broken until 1985, has seen its share of radio audiences drop below 50 per cent. Competition would, no doubt, be even more intense if the government did not prevent radio operators from changing their programming formats in response to new competitive opportunities.

The Government's Entry Blockade

The fundamental limitation on competition within the electronic media has been the government's licensing policy. A publisher wishing to start a new magazine or newspaper does not need a government licence. For a would-be broadcaster (or supplier of cable-TV service), the story is quite different. By restricting the number of television and radio licences it grants, the government creates absolute barriers to new entry – in effect, an entry blockade.

These barriers not only limit competition among current operators, but also remove the threat of potential entry, which can be as important as actual competition in motivating media suppliers to perform well. Poor products or extortionate prices can be quickly exploited by eager entrants when entry barriers are low. In radio, a large number of licences has now been issued, with none of the operators other than the BBC having a substantial share of the radio audience. Nonetheless,

---

but the average customer pays more than £20 once the cost of premium channels is added. In the case of satellite, the hardware costs anywhere from £100 to £250, in addition to a £50 to £80 installation fee and monthly charges. For BSkyB, the UK's largest satellite supplier, those charges range from £11 to £26, depending on how many premium channels are ordered.

radio would be more competitive still if licensing policy did not eliminate the threat of new entry.

For television, the government's entry blockade is a more serious matter. Not until 1955 did the government decide to license the private sector to provide a TV channel, Channel 3 (ITV). Twenty-five more years passed before Channel 4, a quasi-public organisation, was licensed to provide a national service, thus bringing the number of terrestrial channels to four, of which only one is private.

The government's traditional excuse for blocking new entry into electronic media has been that no further spectrum is available. That explanation is no more convincing today than it was in radio's earliest days when the government, having licensed three broadcasters, informed a fourth applicant that 'the ether [spectrum] is already full'.[14] Refusing to license private-sector operators allowed the government to maintain its monopoly over broadcasting, an objective enthusiastically supported not only by the BBC but also by newspapers, which had no desire to compete with broadcasters for advertising.

The emergence of cable TV technology and, before it, radio relay (the radio equivalent) provided a test of the government's real objectives in blocking new broadcasters. Cable television and radio relay distribute signals through wires or cables from the relay operator to homes, making no demands upon the 'ether'. Nevertheless, radio relay operators were prohibited from developing programming themselves to supplement the BBC signals they retransmitted. Similarly, the government initially restricted cable television operators to simultaneous retransmission of other signals, which in effect meant distributing only the BBC and ITV, thus retarding cable TV's development by at least a decade. Blocking entry of new programme suppliers could not be blamed on a putative lack of spectrum, so reasons to block entry were constructed around morality and public convenience. It fell to the Director General of the BBC to pronounce that 'the BBC does not...accept that cable operators should be licensed to interrupt the entertainment patterns of network television'.[15] It is telling that, when broadband cable TV was eventually permitted in Britain, it was advanced not as a broadcasting initiative, but as a matter of industrial policy, aimed at strengthening the technological base of the economy.

---

[14] Eli Noom, *Television in Europe*, Oxford University Press, 1991, p. 16.

[15] *The Times*, 12 October 1982.

The fixed number of broadcast licences at any particular time removes the threat of new terrestrial entry as a restraining influence on the behaviour of existing TV suppliers. Similar obstacles are placed in the way of delivery of TV channels through landline distribution systems (cable TV and telephone networks). The ITC, for example, refuses in principle to license more than one cable system in an area. Its curious justification is that (a) no one would want a second cable licence (if so, the policy is unnecessary), and (b) unless it offered the protection of a statutory cable-TV monopoly, no one would be willing to supply cable service.[16] But the most significant entry barrier is the bar against new terrestrial entry, since terrestrial broadcasting provides the most attractive way of distributing TV programming.

A Spectrum Market ... or Liberalisation of Licensing?

The prospects for significantly increasing the number of operators in the electronic media are mixed. The government could allow a spectrum market to emerge, permitting new broadcasters to offer television and radio services provided they bid more for the spectrum than those who would put it to non-broadcasting uses. The number of broadcast licences would then be determined by impartial market forces, instead of politicians or Whitehall mandarins. The Department of Trade and Industry has, on several occasions, nodded approvingly at the idea of a spectrum market, but nothing practical has come of it.

As long as the government retains its control over entry, the most that can be hoped for is some liberalisation of licensing policy. It remains to be seen whether significant new competition will emerge from the Government's recently announced plans to license more terrestrial TV channels. In addition to the recent awarding of a licence for Channel 5, the Department of National Heritage (DNH) has announced an ambitious programme to assign new television spectrum to operators willing to invest in digital transmission.

Neither effort to create new TV channels is assured of success, because the offers of new spectrum have unappealing conditions attached to them. Consider first the spectrum allocated to Channel 5. It could interfere with transmissions in neighbouring countries, and also

---

[16] The Independent Television Commission, *Memorandum by the Independent Television Commission to the Trade and Industry Select Committee on Optical Fibre Networks*, 24 May 1994, p. 5, para.19.

with the operation of VCRs, so the channel will be limited to an area containing less than 70 per cent of the population and the operator is expected to have to spend some £70 million on retuning VCRs.[17] When the channel was offered the first time, it did not inspire great investor interest. A second offering attracted four bids, and in October 1995 the licence was awarded to Channel 5 Broadcasting, a consortium composed of Pearson, MAI, Compagnie Luxembourgeoise de Télédiffusion, and Warburg Pincus.[18]

The spectrum that is to be made available for digitally compressed transmission of television programming could lead to a significant expansion of the number of terrestrial broadcasters. But current licensees seem to have no strong incentive to invest in a more costly technology that, in the long run, would create more competition for them. Whether newcomers are willing to make the large investments required to transmit digitally compressed signals is not as yet obvious.

Even if no expansion of terrestrial channels occurs soon, the competition provided by cable and satellite channels will continue to grow. Cable-TV penetration so far has been relatively low (around 20 per cent in most areas), and the financial performance of cable television also continues to be disappointing.[19] Nevertheless, investors – now primarily American telephone companies – continue to pump millions of pounds into constructing new cable systems and upgrading the programming available on cable TV. Abolishing monopoly cable TV licences would provide an additional stimulus to lethargic licensees and create an opportunity for more efficient operators to enter their service territory.

The outlook for more satellite television competition seems more promising, but also more complex. It has enough spectrum to expand significantly the number of satellite-delivered channels. And unlike cable television, satellite TV appears to be generating profits. As a practical matter, therefore, it may offer the best prospect for an intensification of television competition.

---

[17] Independent Television Commission, 'Improved Coverage for Channel 5', News Release, 16 March 1995.

[18] Independent Television Commission, 'ITC Announces Its Decision to Award Channel 5 Licence', News Release, 27 October 1995.

[19] In the fourth quarter of 1995, broadband cable penetration stood at 22 per cent. Broadband cable passes just over 6 million homes, of which 1,327,000 subscribe. (*Source*: *New Media Markets*, Vol. 14, No. 8, 29 February 1996, p.I.)

Encryption and Natural Monopoly

The rate of entry of new, competing satellite channels, however, could depend on developments in the market for encryption. That is not true of satellite channels supported entirely by advertising, which have little incentive to encrypt their signals since broadcasting 'in the clear' maximises the viewers they can offer to advertisers. But most satellite channels rely to some extent upon subscription revenue, which necessitates a mechanism for excluding non-subscribers. Cable TV systems have closed distribution systems, but broadcasters must use encryption.

The supply of encryption systems is highly competitive, in the fundamental sense that many encryption technologies compete intensely in a global market-place. But if a single encryption standard comes to be adopted by most consumers, it can be difficult in the short run for competing standards to obtain a foothold in the market.

Encryption may therefore have attributes of a natural monopoly in the short run. The market may tend at any particular time to adopt a single encryption system from the many competing encryption technologies, if the coexistence of several systems in the market-place increases significantly the combined cost to consumers and TV service providers of encryption. That could occur, for example, if each rival system requires a separate decoder (forcing households to acquire multiple decoders in order to subscribe to competing TV services), or if a decoder capable of accommodating several different encryption systems costs considerably more. In those circumstances, only one encryption system is likely to become widely embodied in consumer hardware. The owner of the encryption technology is then likely to possess short-term market power, leading to high prices for encryption that could restrict the number of subscription TV services transmitted by satellite. Moreover, many fear that a supplier of subscription TV services which also owns a dominant encryption system might discriminate against its rivals in its encryption charges.

While there is a real danger that the charges of a dominant encryption system would reduce the entry of new satellite channels, concern that a TV service might use its control of encryption to discriminate against competing TV services is greatly exaggerated. The notion that a company would 'leverage' its monopoly in encryption to develop a monopoly in the market for programming services is fallacious, because doing so would not increase its profits. The owner of an encryption monopoly can extract whatever profits are available in the programming market by setting the encryption charges at appropriate levels, and the resulting profits cannot be improved upon by integrating downstream and driving out competitors.[20]

Leveraging in the opposite direction, however, could be profitable. The supplier of popular subscription TV services may, by virtue of its position in the programme market, succeed in having its encryption system adopted as the industry standard. There is, however, no convincing reason to believe that a dominant encryption system poses any greater problem when owned by a competitor in the downstream programming market than by an independent vendor.

The behaviour observed in encryption markets seems consistent with these expectations. It is not unusual for the encryption technology employed by the largest supplier of subscription TV services to become dominant. That has happened in France and Germany, where Canal Plus and the Kirsch Group have their own popular encryption technologies. BSkyB, the UK's largest supplier of satellite television services, has the exclusive licence for Videocrypt,[21] which has become the dominant encryption system here. But there is no apparent evidence of price discrimination against competing channel providers. Charges for Videocrypt are posted on a published rate card that does not distinguish between BSkyB and competing suppliers of subscription TV services.[22] Moreover, no one has reportedly been deterred from offering a satellite-transmitted TV service because of Videocrypt's charges.

Some TV operators, however, have elected to have their channels incorporated in a BSkyB programme package, rather than offering the channels independently and paying Videocrypt's charges. As a result, the public may have been deprived of price competition that otherwise would have occurred among pay channels.

Encryption provides a useful reminder of regulation's limitations. The mere fact that an encryption technology becomes dominant reveals

---

20 It is well established in the literature that, when the service produced by an upstream monopoly is used in fixed input portions in the downstream market, and the downstream market is characterised by competitive cost conditions, the upstream producer has no profit incentive to leverage its monopoly into the downstream market. Thus, anti-competitive discrimination in pricing encryption services should not occur, unless economic actors behave irrationally.

21 Videocrypt is owned by News International, which also owns 40 per cent of BSkyB.

22 Charges do vary, of course, with the number of channels that a service provider wishes to encrypt. But, in the terminology of Pigou, no third-degree discrimination occurs: any two programmers demanding identical encryption services will be charged the same.

nothing about whether a competition problem exists. If the cost of switching to a rival encryption system is negligible, a dominant encryption provider will have no real market power, since any effort to increase encryption charges would simply trigger substitution of some other encryption system(s) by service providers and consumers. But suppose instead that switching from one encryption to another could be quite costly. The government then might impose decoder hardware standards to facilitate competition among encryption systems, as the EC has considered doing. Such efforts, however, could do more harm than good. Governmental standard-setting delays the introduction of new technology; moreover, encryption suppliers could succeed in capturing the standard-setting process and turning it to their own advantage. Thus, government-imposed standards could lead to more concentration than if the government chose not to intervene.

Instead of standard-setting, the competition authorities might declare a dominant encryption system an 'essential facility', and regulate the terms on which suppliers of TV service have access to it. Recent experience provides a reminder, however, that even regulating the prices of basic commodities like electricity and natural gas is very difficult to do well. Regulating encryption services would be far more challenging. The costs of encryption could not be established with much precision, nor could the profit necessary to preserve incentives to invest in developing new encryption technology.[23]

The best solution probably resides in the long-run competition among encryption technologies that will inevitably continue and be likely to intensify. The market power inherent in any technology is quickly eroded, and encryption is no exception. Within the next year or so, most satellite operators plan to convert to digital transmission, which will necessitate replacing current encryption technologies, including Videocrypt. Already, an alliance of powerful media interests (including companies now being carried on a BSkyB package, as well as such major American backers as Viacom and Ted Turner's CNN) has formed to develop a new, rival encryption system. The outcome could be two major encryption systems competing side by side, with decoders

---

[23] Developing a successful encryption system involves significant investment in R&D, and many efforts fail – the equivalent of oil explorers drilling dry holes. To preserve incentives for firms to develop new and better encryption systems, regulation would need to hold out the prospect of compensating the owner of a dominant encryption system for R&D costs, as well as direct costs, *and* a profit commensurate with the risks of attempting to develop new technology. It is unrealistic to suppose that regulation could do that satisfactorily.

equipped to handle both, and numerous other encryption systems waiting in the wings.

All this suggests that television, the one media segment still characterised by relatively few service suppliers, will see a continuing influx of new competitors. Growth in the number of providers of satellite services seems inevitable, and with it the number of households willing to make the investment necessary to receive satellite TV. Cable television may also become a greater force in the market if its efforts to improve programming are successful and its marketing and pricing strategies are improved. The greatest fillip to competition, however, would come from creating a spectrum market allowing all broadcasters – current as well as potential – to bid on as much spectrum as they choose rather than being limited to the spectrum currently licensed for TV use.

Media Influence

Principles of Measurement

Determining a media company's political and cultural influence presents unusually difficult problems of measurement. Revenue, ordinarily used in assessing a company's economic power, does not provide a useful guide because much of it comes from advertising. Advertising revenue reflects advertisers' willingness to pay to reach audiences with particular demographic characteristics, not the media's political and cultural influence.

The latter might seem to be revealed by consumer expenditures on the media – revenue from newspaper sales, subscriptions to television channels and so forth. But that also has a fatal flaw. Some media (for instance, Channels 3 and 4) obtain no revenue from subscriptions, and so by that measure would be assigned zero market shares. By contrast, some media rely entirely on revenue from consumers. A media company's mix of revenues from consumers and advertisers reflects institutional restraints or a business decision of how best to recoup costs, and cannot be expected to provide a reliable indicator of public influence. Moreover, measuring media influence by consumer expenditures would give undue weight to those prepared to spend more on their media choices. That is a serious defect, since concern about media influence is egalitarian in nature.

There is a natural measure of influence that avoids these pitfalls. It is the time – rather than the money – that the public spends on various media. Measuring the concentration of potential media influence becomes a matter of determining whether a few media companies attract an inordinate share of the time the public spends on the media. The measure is intuitively appealing, because the potential influence of a magazine, a television channel or a newspaper should be correlated with the time the public spends on it. The correlation, no doubt, is imperfect. But some imprecision is unavoidable: directly measuring a media product's influence on public opinion would confront intractable problems. Not least is establishing causation. Do the media chosen by people influence their beliefs, or do their beliefs influence the media they choose? As a practical matter, therefore, the potential to influence public opinion seems best assessed by examining how people distribute their time over the media. But this raises some methodological issues that must first be resolved.

Whose Influence: Gatekeeper or Author?

The defining rôle of the media is to disseminate information. But many media companies also produce much of the material they disseminate. Television channels exhibit a mix of internally produced programming and programming commissioned and produced by others. Similarly, newspapers and magazines typically publish articles written by their own staffs and pieces acquired from outsiders.

The dual rôle of 'gatekeeper' and producer of much of the material distributed raises an important question – which activity should be used in gauging media influence? The answer will determine, for example, whether the audience for a cable television channel is ascribed to the company producing the programme service or to the owners of the local cable systems that distribute it.

It seems more useful to measure concentration at the gatekeeper rather than the producer level. Concerns commonly expressed about media influence centre on gatekeeping. There is no evidence of a dearth of writers or would-be programme producers; rather, the question is whether they can gain reasonable access to the public. Concentration is far less likely to occur at the creation stage than in distribution, where economies of scale and scope may favour the formation of large enterprises. Moreover, assigning audience to the company that creates material rather than to the company distributing it would almost certainly result in lower measured concentration. Thus, measuring concentration at the dissemination level – the media as gatekeepers – produces a more exacting test. If no concentration problem is discovered there, it seems safe to assume no concentration problem occurs at the upstream stage of creating the material.

There is one special circumstance, however, where a limited departure from attributing audience to gatekeepers seems advisable. It entails passive retransmissions of material distributed by other gatekeepers. Although cable television systems are developing more of their own programming, the terrestrial channels (the BBC, Channel 3 and Channel 4) and BSkyB still account for much of the audiences they attract. It seems appropriate to attribute the cable television audiences for such passive retransmissions to the primary broadcasters.

Influence on What?

It is impossible to think of a subject not covered in some way by the media. Such staples as politics and political commentary share pages and airwaves with opera and opera criticism, gossip, philosophy, science and business. In each area, there are critics who complain that the media exert a malign influence, most commonly in politics. A political party may blame defeat at the polls on biased coverage by a few large media groups; political fringe groups routinely complain they cannot obtain a fair hearing because of the media's vested interests in the *status quo*. Complaints are not limited to political matters. For example, producers of *avant-garde* art object that they cannot gain public exposure because the mass media cater to bourgeois taste.

Whether these and other examples of alleged media influence, constitute problems from society's perspective – let alone problems attributable to concentration – is much disputed. Whatever the subject, matters of little interest to the public will inevitably be given limited coverage by the mass media. Demands made on the media to inform the public on matters of limited interest will always exceed society's capacity to satisfy them.

The relevant question is not whether all speakers seeking access to the media always succeed in being widely heard (they do not and cannot), but whether concentration in the media creates a serious risk that the flow of information consumed by the public is unnecessarily restricted. To answer that question, one might try to examine media concentration in each of a number of subject areas – politics and current affairs, political philosophy, business and economics, the arts, the sciences.

Disaggregation by subject area, however, is impractical. A newspaper, a magazine or a television channel presents content spanning a broad range of subjects. Although considerable information is available on the total time individuals spend on particular media, it is rarely disaggregated by subject matter. For example, the time people spend reading individual newspapers is known, but how that time is distributed over current affairs, gardening, the arts and sport is not. Television, and sometimes radio, may seem exceptions, because programme-specific audiences are estimated. But classifying individual programmes by subject area would frequently require an exercise of judgement that would be troublingly arbitrary.

The Aggregate Market-Place for Information

These considerations suggest looking instead at the aggregate market-place for information. Aggregate media concentration could overstate or understate the media concentration that arises in connection with a particular subject area, if the mix of content varies significantly across media companies. Superficially, such disparities seem to exist. Television and cinema are often equated with entertainment; newspapers with news; and magazines with special subject areas. Yet these seemingly sharp differences begin to blur on closer examination. Most popular media products, whether print or electronic, provide a broad content mix, ranging from news and current affairs to entertainment. General entertainment TV programming often contains readily discernible political undercurrents and points of view, while tabloid coverage of current politics often provides as much entertainment as fact. Thus, concentration in the overall market for information seems a reasonable measure of individual companies' influence in particular areas.

There will inevitably be some circumstances under which any methodology for measuring media concentration will produce counter-intuitive results. The appropriate test of a methodology, therefore, is whether, under the range of circumstances likely to be experienced, it produces an accurate depiction of potential influence. Our proposal for calculating media differs, for example, from that submitted by the British Media Industry Group (BMIG) to the Department of National Heritage.[24] Our measure is simple and direct: the total time the public spends on a company's media products relative to the time it spends on all media products. It could produce anomalous results if one media

[24] British Media Industry Group, 'A New Approach to Cross-Media Ownership,' mimeo, February 1995. The BMIG is composed of Associated Newspapers Ltd., Pearson plc, The Guardian Group plc, and The Telegraph plc.

segment were extremely concentrated. For example, if a single company owned every national newspaper in the country, its share of total media use would be that accounted for by national newspapers, currently about 7 per cent. Yet that would understate the concern that would be felt if all national newspapers were published by a single company.

BMIG's measure of concentration, like ours, is based on consumer use of the media. But it proposes calculating each company's 'share of voice' as a weighted average of its *share* of each of four media segments: (1) national newspapers, (2) regional and local newspapers, (3) all television and (4) radio. The BMIG measure would be identical to ours if it used as weights the proportion of total media use accounted for by each segment. But BMIG assigns identical weights to each segment, regardless of its relative importance. (The exception, radio, is given only half the normal weight.) Equal weights may evoke the notion of parity and thus sound 'fair'. But since there is no objective respect in which the media segments defined by BMIG are equal, assigning them equal weights is not only arbitrary but misleading.

Moreover, equal weights would not prevent anomalous results if media segments were highly concentrated. A company with a monopoly in television, which most people designate as the most reliable source of news, would be assigned an overall share of only 28 per cent by BMIG, even though capturing 60 per cent of all media use. Our measure would assign a share of 60 per cent, reflecting television's dominance in media use.

But the performance of concentration measures under extreme circumstances is essentially irrelevant, because the normal functioning of competition policy would prevent any media segment from becoming extremely concentrated.[25] The pertinent question is whether a

---

[25] That is particularly so because the Monopolies and Mergers Commission (MMC) tends to define markets quite narrowly (often implausibly so). In its 1993 report *The Supply of National Newspapers*, for example, the MMC not only dismisses the notion that television competes in the same market as newspapers, but even manages to reach the baffling conclusion that they are complements, which would mean that an increase in newspaper prices would cause consumers to watch less television: '[W]e take [television] more as a complement to newspapers than a substitute product, at least for the majority of consumers' (p. 8, para.3.5). The Commission further asserted that regional newspapers do not compete significantly with nationals: 'For the most part ... the regionalised elements of national newspapers are limited to sports coverage and television listings. Moreover, regional newspapers by their nature focus on news which is primarily of local and regional interest and most consumers wanting national and international news will usually purchase a national newspaper' (p. 8, para.3.5). The MMC even questioned whether quality newspapers compete with tabloids, noting that 'quality titles

method for computing concentration provides a meaningful measure in the actual media environment, as it exists now and is likely to evolve. By that test, it is difficult to think of a more satisfactory measure of a media company's influence than the proportion of consumers' time it succeeds in attracting. Of course, assigning parity to every hour of media use could be challenged on the grounds that some media provide a more intense experience than other media, and that the mix of content varies across media in ways that might enter into the construction of an ideal index. Nevertheless, concerns about media influence are not limited to a single area such as news coverage, and trying to assign individual weights to each of the media to reflect their intrinsic importance is not only time-consuming, but arbitrary and contentious. Indeed, the controversies generated by arbitrary weighting assignments can be imagined from BMIG's methodology. It would treat possession of a 30 per cent share of TV viewing as no more consequential than a 30 per cent share of regional newspaper circulation, even though the public exposure obtained by the TV operator would be more than 25 times larger.

Any cross-media index of influence may produce anomalous results if a particular media segment is highly concentrated. But the share of the total time the public spends on the media provides a direct, intuitively appealing measure of the extent to which any media company is in a position to exert undue influence on the public's views, values and attitudes.

The Data

The most comprehensive single source of information on media use is the National Readership Survey (NRS). The survey encompasses electronic media (television and radio) and cinema, as well as print media (newspapers and magazines). A large sample of the population is randomly selected and each respondent is interviewed in person, providing more accurate results than telephone interviews or mail

are almost twice the price of popular titles, ... the breadth and depth of coverage is undoubtedly greater, and the range of news items, particularly those dealing with international stories, is generally more extensive' (pp. 8-9, para.3.7). The first of these considerations, the price differentiation between tabloids and broadsheets, is simply irrelevant to whether they are substitutes, as any beginning student of economics should know. If, for example, a 20-ounce box of soap sells for twice the price of a 10-ounce box, a consumer will normally find the two sizes highly substitutable, despite the price differential. The report did eventually conclude, however, that quality papers and tabloids do *not* represent 'distinct economic markets' (p. 9, para.3.8).

surveys. The interview, which typically takes two hours to administer, covers each national newspaper, 19 regional newspapers, more than 200 magazines and all radio, television and cinema.

The National Readership Survey has several important virtues for the purpose of measuring the public's use of the media. Many media audits, such as the British Audience Research Board (BARB) sample used to estimate TV audiences, are limited to a single medium. Although individual media audits can be combined, mixing different samples can produce misleading conclusions. A more reliable profile of media use is obtained by surveying the same set of people about each of the media, as the NRS does. That also makes it possible to examine how the patronage of individual media products is interrelated – for example, whether the television viewing habits of *The Guardian* readers differ from readers of *The Daily Express* or *The Sunday Times*. That information is valuable because, even if concentration is low for the population as a whole, there may be particular groups whose media use implies significant concentration.

A no less important advantage of the NRS is the very large group it surveys. Most studies of media consumption rely on relatively small samples of the population. The BARB audit of television viewing uses one of the larger samples, whose size is still less than 5,000. Using the NRS, we examined the media use of over 30,000 adults over the year ending April 1992. These data were updated to the year ending April 1994 by incorporating intervening aggregate trends in the circulation of individual newspapers and audiences for radio and television services. The results should provide a highly reliable picture of the media use of the population as a whole.

The measures of media use provided by the NRS differ between print and electronic media.

- *Newspapers and Magazines* – For each newspaper and magazine title, survey respondents are asked whether they ever read it and, if so, with what frequency and when they last read an issue. The NRS does not routinely survey people about how long they spend reading individual publications, but that information is available from other sources.[26]

- *Radio and Television* – Respondents are asked how much time they spend with radio and television over the course of a typical week

[26] For example, data on the duration of magazine reading, by type, can be found in The Magazine Marketplace Group, *Median Reading Time by Publication*, and IPC Magazines, *Media Values*.

and how that time is distributed among BBC and other radio and television services.

Using these data, the total time each respondent spends on the media in a typical week can be estimated, and how that time is distributed over individual media products. By combining those data with information on media ownership, each company's share of the time people spend on the media can be determined.[27]

Our compilations reflect two notable omissions. *First*, the NRS survey is limited to 19 of the approximately 90 regional daily newspapers and includes none of the hundreds of local newspapers. *Second*, our compilation of magazine reading is quite limited. Of over 200 magazines covered by the survey, most are read by only a small fraction of the population. Each title included in the analysis adds significantly to the computation burden. As a practical matter, therefore, our analysis of magazine readership is limited to the top 20 weekly and top 20 monthly magazines, as measured by circulation. They account for a large portion of magazine readership, which constitutes a relatively minor share of total media use. The effect of omitting these minor regional newspapers and magazines could be some overstatement of media concentration.

Analysing Media Concentration and Influence

Concentration in the national media market is relevant to such broad questions as whether individual companies are in a position to exert undue influence on general public opinion or the outcome of national elections. But it may also be useful to consider the concentration of media use within the population: some groups, for example, might spend a disproportionate amount of time with the media products of only a few companies. Therefore, in addition to analysing media con-

---

27 Ownership interests in media operations are continually changing hands. After our extensive tabulation of the time spent by the public on individual electronic and print media, a number of media properties changed hands, necessitating an updating of ownership information. We attempted to reflect all transactions completed by 1 June 1994 that could have a noticeable effect on the measured media concentration. For example, we incorporated Pearson's increase in its holdings of BSkyB from 14·7 per cent to 17·5 per cent, as well as such major changes as Carlton's acquisition of Central. But we did not reflect pending transactions that had not been completed by 1 June, such as The Daily Mail and General Trust's acquisition of MAI's radio holdings, or the effect of BSkyB's recent public flotation.

TABLE 2:
National Media Use, by Media Segment, 1993-94

Media Segment	Per Capita Weekly Hours	Per cent
Television		
BBC	11·2	28·1
Commercial (ITV + Channel 4)	12·9	32·3
Radio		
BBC	6·3	15·7
Commercial	5·1	12·8
Newspaper		
National Dailies	1·5	3·7
National Sunday	1·3	3·3
Regionals	0·7	1·8
Magazines		
Top 20 Weeklies	0·6	1·6
Top 20 Monthlies	0·2	0·4
Cinema	0·1	0·2
TOTAL	39·9	100·0*

• Numbers do not sum to 100% due to rounding.

Source: William B. Shew, 'U.K. Media Concentration' (mimeo), July 1994.

Centration for the population as a whole, we have also examined the media use of several groups.

The National Market

The average adult in the UK spends almost 40 hours per week on the media[28] (see Table 2). Over 60 per cent is television viewing, slightly more than half of which is commercial television. Radio listening represents about 28 per cent. Newspapers and magazines account, res-

[28] Because our calculations exclude some regional newspapers, all local newspapers, and less popular magazines, total media use is actually somewhat higher.

TABLE 3:
National Media Concentration

Company	Media Use per cent
BBC	44·1
Carlton Communication	6.9
Channel Four Television Corporation	6·2
Granada Television Ltd	4·1
Capital Radio Investments Ltd	3·4
News International plc	3·4
MAI plc	3·0
Yorkshire Television Holdings plc	2·5
Mirror Group Newspapers	2·0
HTV Group	1·8
Scottish Television plc	1·4
Daily Mail and General Trust plc	1·1
United Newspapers plc	1·0
Pearson plc	0·9
Reed Elsevier plc	0·8
EMAP plc	0·8
Luxembourg Telecom Company	0·7
D.C. Thompson and Company Ltd	0·5
Television South West plc	0·5
WH Smith Ltd	0·5
Guardian Media Group	0·5
Transworld Communications	0·5
LBC Radio Group	0·5
CM Black Investments	0·4
GWR Group	0·3
H. Bauer Verlag	0·3
Border Television plc	0·3
Thomas Investments Ltd	0·3
Time Warner International	0·3
Sir Peter Michael	0·3
Grampian Television plc	0·2
Radio Clyde Holdings	0·2
Ulster VC plc	0·2
Metro Goldwyn Meyer	0·1
Sports Newspapers	0·1
Newspaper Publishing plc	0·1
Chiltern Radio	0·1
East Anglian Radio Group	0·1
Gruner & Jahr, Bertlesmann, Constanze	0·1
GMTV	0·1
All Others	9·4
TOTAL	100·0

Source: William B. Shew, 'U.K. Media Concentration' (mimeo), July 1994.

Pectively, for approximately 9 and 2 per cent. Cinema accounts for less than 1 per cent.

This dominance of the electronic media is striking. In part, it may be related to the commonly observed preference among the young for television and radio rather than the printed word. And the public's growing insistence on obtaining information as quickly as possible gives the electronic media a competitive edge.

The public's distribution of its media use over companies is somewhat surprising. The media conglomerates often criticised for their size have inconsequential shares of the national media market. (See Table 3). Carlton Communications, now the largest private sector media company as measured by the expenditure of consumers' time, accounts for less than 7 per cent of media use. The next largest private sector enterprise, Granada, accounts for just over 4 per cent.

Two of the three largest media enterprises are public-sector entities – the BBC and Channel 4. The BBC, by far the larger, is the only company with a significant share of the national media market. Its share of 44 per cent is not unexpected, given the number of television and radio services it supplies and the government's licensing policy. Channel 4 accounts for over 6 per cent of media use.

Channel 4 has a higher share of the national market than most ITV companies because it is a national television service, whereas Channel 3 is a regional service, with most of the regions served by independently owned companies. Since ITV stations collectively decide on network programming (which accounts for most transmissions of the individual stations) it might seem that, at least for the network components, all ITV broadcasters ought to be treated as a single entity. But there is a powerful rationale for treating the ITV franchises not under common ownership as separate entities. Concentration is being measured at the gatekeeper level, and each individual franchise is free to determine what programmes are aired on its station, including the amount of network programming.[29]

By conventional standards the share data presented in Table 3 do not portray a highly concentrated industry. Indeed, putting aside public sector broadcasting, the market-place for information in the UK appears highly competitive, containing numerous firms, with even the largest accounting for a negligible market share.

---

[29] Moreover, audiences for the network component of TV broadcasting would in any event be attributed to regional ITV companies, since they are the network owners.

Joint Ownership

Often a media product – a newspaper, a television service – is jointly owned by several companies. The share figures presented in Table 3 impute to each owner of a media product the time people spend on it in proportion to his ownership interest. Thus Pearson is assigned 17·5 per cent of the hours spent by the public watching BSkyB channels, since it owned 17·5 per cent of BSkyB during the period examined.

It might be argued, however, that only the majority ownership interest in a media product is relevant in assessing media concentration: the majority owner may be able to override the preferences of its partners, and so operate as the sole gatekeeper. That would suggest assigning all of the audience to the company with a majority ownership interest, imputing no audience share to other owners.

Calculating shares in that way, though, does not produce any significant changes. Assigning all audience to the majority owner increases the national market shares of Yorkshire Television and News International by about a percentage point each. The market shares of most companies change by a fraction of a percentage point, if at all. The national media market-place is quite unconcentrated, whichever measure is adopted.

Differential Weighting of Media Use

Should an hour spent reading a newspaper or magazine be given greater weight than an hour spent watching television or going to the cinema? The electronic media and cinema may be regarded as less consequential than print media because of their content mix, or because reading represents a more active engagement and thus perhaps is more influential. We therefore examined how our conclusions would be affected if one hour spent on print media is accorded as much importance as two hours spent on non-print media. Measured concentration is little changed by that assumption. The BBC's share of the national media market slips from 44 per cent to 40 per cent. The shares of other media enterprises change significantly less. There is even less concentration in the media market if time spent on print media is regarded as more important than the same time spent on non-print media.

Concentration among Particular User Groups: Guardian and Sun Readers

Even though the national media market-place is quite unconcentrated, some significant concentration might occur in the media use of specific

TABLE 4:
Use by Media Segment, *Guardian* Readers, 1993-94

Media Segment	Per Capita Weekly Hours	Per cent
Television		
BBC	8·7	28·7
Commercial	7·7	25·1
Radio		
BBC	3·8	12·3
Commercial	3·2	10·3
Newspaper		
National Dailies	3·8	12·3
National Sunday	1·8	5·7
Regionals	0·7	2·2
Magazines		
Top 20 Weeklies	0·6	1·9
Top 20 Monthlies	0·3	0·9
Cinema	0·2	0·5
TOTAL	30·8	100·0*

- Numbers do not sum to 100% due to rounding.

Source: William B. Shew, 'U.K. Media Concentration' (mimeo), July 1994.

Groups within the population. To test this possibility, we looked at two groups one would expect to be dissimilar: regular readers of *The Guardian* and regular readers of *The Sun*.

Regular *Guardian* readers are relatively light users of media, spending 9 hours less per week than the national average (see Table 4). They spend considerably less time on television and radio than the average person, but somewhat more on newspapers.

The overall concentration of media use among *Guardian* readers is not substantially different from national media concentration. Guardian Media Group, owner of *The Guardian*, accounts for a much higher share of the media used by this group (8·1 per cent compared with 0·5 per cent in Table 3), as one would expect. On the other hand,

TABLE 5:
Use by Media Segment, *Sun* Readers, 1993-94

Media Segment	Per Capita Weekly Hours	Per cent
Television		
BBC	12·0	23·4
Commercial	15·8	30·9
Radio		
BBC	9·1	17·8
Commercial	7·4	14·5
Newspaper		
National Dailies	3·1	6·1
National Sunday	1·9	3·7
Regionals	0·8	1·5
Magazines		
Top 20 Weeklies	0·8	1·5
Top 20 Monthlies	0·2	0·4
Cinema	0·1	0·2
TOTAL	51·2	100·0

Source: William B. Shew, 'U.K. Media Concentration' (mimeo), July 1994.

the BBC's share drops from 44·1 to 41 per cent, consistent with *Guardian* readers' lighter use of television.

Sun readers are relatively heavy media users, spending over 25 per cent more time on the media than the national average (see Table 5). They spend more time on almost every media segment.

Media concentration among *Sun* readers differs only slightly from concentration among the general population: the share of the BBC is a few percentage points lower among *Sun* readers, while the share of News International, which owns *The Sun*, is a few points higher.

Comparison of the general population with regular readers of *The Sun* and *The Guardian* provides some basis for ascertaining more generally whether media concentration is likely to be significantly greater among particular groups than for the population as a whole. Despite their different demographic characteristics, the media-use patterns of the two groups examined here differ little from those of the general population. Although the BBC accounts for a slightly lower proportion of media use among regular readers of both *The Sun* and *The Guardian*, compared to the population as a whole, the differences are never more than a few percentage points. The comparisons provide no evidence that media concentration is likely to be significantly greater within particular groups than for the population at large.

Concentration: Conclusions

Concerns have been expressed that the market-place for ideas exhibits a troubling level of concentration, that large media companies may wield too much influence, warranting remedial government action. Our detailed examination of the media consumption choices of over 30,000 people suggests that such concerns are ill-founded. Most people seem to patronise media products owned by a wide array of companies. Only one, the BBC, can claim a large share of the national market, accounting for slightly over 44 per cent. Carlton Communications, the largest private sector media company, accounts for less than 7 per cent of national media use. Channel 4, a public-sector enterprise, accounts for just over 6 per cent. Of the remaining media companies, the largest has a share slightly higher than 4 per cent. By conventional standards, the media industry seems quite unconcentrated. That conclusion is left unaltered if one hour spent on the print media is deemed as important as two hours spent on electronic media, or if, for media with joint owners, all use is assigned to the majority owner.

Concerns about concentration among particular groups within the population also appear without foundation. The media use of the two groups we examined is surprisingly similar to the profile for the country as a whole. Some companies enjoy slightly larger shares of the media use by those groups; other companies slightly smaller. But the media market appears no more concentrated for these groups than for the general population.

In summary, the media market is quite diverse and unconcentrated by conventional standards, with even the largest private sector companies accounting for a negligible share of national media use. Nor are there signs that this unconcentrated, diverse structure is under threat. Indeed, all evidence points in the opposite direction. Even the BBC – the only organisation with a large market share – has seen that share steadily eroded by the emergence of cable and satellite TV companies, and the rapid growth of private sector radio stations. The last dozen years have also seen the entry of nine new national newspapers, of which four have survived, and a revitalisation of the regional press. There are now 90 daily and nearly 1,500 weekly regional newspapers, with a combined circulation of nearly 45 million and advertising revenues which exceed those of national papers. New magazines proliferate. All these trends point towards increasing competition and diversity. So the notion that regulation must be reformulated to deal with a crisis posed by high or increasing media concentration is, on examination, quite unconvincing.

Media Cross-Ownership

The current demand to reassess the regulation of media ownership, though, stems partly from the 'convergence' expected from advances in media technology. Media companies fear existing government restrictions will prevent them from taking full advantage of the technological opportunities now being opened. Government watchdogs are concerned that the companies may be too successful, with the result that the industry will become controlled by a few media conglomerates.

Economies of Cross-Ownership?

Cross-ownership is scarcely new. Its pervasiveness is explained by the frequent opportunities to realise economies from bringing several media operations under common ownership. Where economies of integration are significant, integration becomes necessary to survive in the market-place.

Could these economies be realised without resorting to cross-ownership? It might be argued that whatever co-operation is necessary to achieve them could be arranged through contracts, perhaps involving strategic alliances or joint ventures. In many cases, that is true – witness the large number of such arrangements in the industry. But those alternative arrangements are not a good substitute for cross-ownership where the activity to be co-ordinated is complex and involves many uncertainties. The costs of transactions between separately owned companies would then be high, and the co-ordination that results would tend to fall short of what could be achieved through cross-ownership.

Cross-Ownership and Concentration

But unrestrained pursuit of the potential efficiency gains from integration raises the possibility of cross-ownership so extensive that a troubling increase in concentration occurs. The question thus arises of how cross-ownership can best be regulated to ensure that a few companies, in their pursuit of economies of scope, do not come to dominate the media market. At the present time, no evidence of that danger exists. Experience in Britain and elsewhere suggests that some companies are finding economies in operating across media, others are finding such economies elusive, and still others are choosing to specialise in one or a few of the many profitable niches that characterise the media business. But there are now restrictions on media cross-ownership (albeit restrictions that are highly criticised); moreover, the convergence of media, telecommunications and computers may create incentives for more extensive cross-ownership than in the past.

Regulation of Cross-Ownership

The government now regulates cross-ownership in two ways. The competition authorities – the OFT and the MMC – act to ensure that markets remain competitive and that practices do not occur that would operate against the public interest. In addition, special obligations are defined with respect to the media. Mergers of newspapers with a combined circulation exceeding 500,000 are automatically referred to the MMC, which is required to consider, *inter alia*, whether the proposed merger would hamper the 'free expression of opinion'.[30]

The second form of regulation is a set of administrative rules that constrains cross-ownership by establishing numerical limits on ownership shares. The rules, embodied in provisions of the Broadcasting Act 1990, are complex enough in their taxonomy to occupy 15 pages of fine print. They distinguish among Channel 3 regional services, Channel 3 national services, domestic satellite services, non-domestic satellite services, national radio services, local radio services, national newspapers, and local newspapers. The character of the regulations can be conveyed by a few examples. The owner of a national newspaper is prevented from owning more than 20 per cent of any terrestrial TV service or a national radio service. A local newspaper is subjected to the same constraints, except that it can acquire a regional ITV licence that does not significantly overlap the territory served by its newspaper.[31] The owner of a regional ITV licence can obtain no more than a 20 per cent ownership interest in a national Channel 3 service or in the prospective Channel 5.[32]

---

[30] Fair Trading Act 1973, Section 59 (3).

[31] Broadcasting Act 1990, Schedule 2, Part IV, para.2.

[32] Broadcasting Act 1990, Schedule 2, Part III, para.5.

Criticisms of Cross-Ownership Rules

The rigid constraints imposed by these rules have been criticised on two fundamental grounds: *first*, they arbitrarily curb opportunities to achieve efficiencies of integration and, *second*, they distort competition by giving some types of media firms an unfair advantage over their domestic competitors. The first criticism has merit, the second does not.

Consider first the contention that the current rules do not produce a level playing field, insofar as the permitted degree of cross-ownership varies with whether a newspaper is national or local and whether a television service is terrestrial, cable or satellite. The ITV companies claim they are at a competitive disadvantage because they cannot integrate with a national newspaper, whereas a television service provided by direct-to-home (DTH) satellite or by cable can.

That contention, however, overlooks two key points. *First*, if the combination of a non-terrestrial television service and a newspaper offers a competitive advantage over simply providing a terrestrial television service, every media company is free to pursue the former strategy. Unlike terrestrial television, where the number of companies is limited by the government's licensing policy, there is no such constraint limiting the number of companies that can offer a satellite service in conjunction with newspaper publishing. Moreover, the claim that a non-terrestrial TV service owned by a publisher has a competitive advantage over a terrestrial TV licence is implausible. If that were true, it would be difficult to explain the large audience shares obtained by the ITV companies or the extremely high bids made for Channel 3 licences, which reflect the expected profitability of terrestrial television. Thus, the notion that particular companies are put at a competitive disadvantage by media-specific cross-ownership restrictions is groundless. So also is the claim that Channel 3 operators are the weak sisters of cable and satellite services in which newspaper publishers have an ownership interest.

Second, cross-ownership rules must distinguish between local and national newspapers and between terrestrial and non-terrestrial TV services if they are to balance, however crudely, concerns about media concentration on the one hand with the prospective efficiency gains from cross-media ownership. Non-terrestrial TV still accounts for a negligible share of TV viewing, whereas in most areas the Channel 3 franchise accounts for approximately 40 per cent of all viewer hours. If a newspaper were to acquire 100 per cent of a Channel 3 franchise, media concentration would be increased far more than if the same newspaper were to acquire a non-terrestrial TV service. The current rules, by distinguishing various media according to their intrinsic significance – national newspapers loom larger than local newspapers, terrestrial TV services tower over non-terrestrial services – take these disparities into account in defining permissible cross-ownership patterns.

As long as rigid cross-ownership constraints are used to regulate concentration, they must distinguish among types of media to *avoid* competitive distortions. Satellite and cable, as existing policy recognises, are both qualitatively and quantitatively different from terrestrial TV. Permitting a newspaper to acquire a controlling interest in a traditional terrestrial service would have quite different competitive implications from permitting it to own a cable system or a satellite service. If media concentration is to continue to be regulated through administrative rules, those rules have to be structured to reflect the differing importance of the various types of media.

Even though the current rules provide a level playing field for UK media companies, there is still the question of whether UK media companies as a group are placed at a disadvantage relative to their counterparts abroad who are subjected to less stringent regulation of cross-ownership. It is sometimes argued that it is easier abroad to form media conglomerates, which can then enter the UK market and exploit the larger scope and scale of their activities, to obtain a competitive advantage over their UK competitors. And, similarly, when UK media companies attempt to penetrate foreign markets, the same handicap could come into play.

Experience does not always support these contentions. Sony, for example, wishes it had never bought a movie studio and Time Inc. shareholders do not celebrate the anniversary of their marriage to Warner's. But anticipated synergies are real enough in the minds of industry participants to warrant consideration by policy-makers, and to tip the scales in favour of allowing more rather than less freedom to firms seeking to operate across media lines – subject, of course, to preserving a competitive market-place for the exchange of ideas and information.

Improving the Existing Regulatory System

The absence of media concentration and the potential efficiency gains from cross-media ownership do not, of course, dispose of concerns that existing regulatory policy requires updating to account for recent rapid changes in technology and in the intensity of international competition. We start with the premise that a proper policy will not unduly impede industry convergence, in response to consumer choice, but will at the same time preserve and, indeed, encourage a diversity of sources of news, views and entertainment.

Existing policy appears, so far, to have met both objectives. The power of terrestrial broadcasters has declined. More than 3·5 million British households now receive satellite broadcasts on their 'dishes',[33] and another 1·4 million subscribe to cable TV service. The total share of UK television viewing accounted for by cable and satellite channels is about 9 per cent and their share of commercial television advertising revenue is approximately 5 per cent. This leaves the four terrestrial channels with over 90 per cent of viewers, and ITV and Channel 4 with nearly 90 per cent of advertising revenues. The number of radio broadcasters has increased dramatically, and newspaper competition is more intense than ever.

But continuing surveillance of this key industry might be better assigned completely to the competition authorities. They are in a position to analyse, in specific cases, the dangers of increased concentration and balance them against potential efficiency gains. That is precisely the sort of reasoned judgement that competition law is designed to produce. So, in theory at least, replacing administrative rules with greater reliance on competition law should provide a less blunt instrument for governing cross-ownership in the interests of the public.

It might be objected, however, that competition policy can be somewhat erratic; that the media affect the public interest more profoundly than cars or pubs; and that competition law is not well equipped to deal with these broader social ramifications. As for the first of these two objections, the outcome of applying reason and judgement on a case-by-case basis is intrinsically less predictable than applying a mechanical rule, but predictability here is really self-inflicted policy paralysis – the relinquishing of reason. As for the second objection, the competition authorities could be instructed to attach a higher value to competition in media markets than is customary in other markets when evaluating the 'public interest', and to recognise the particular desirability of low concentration in the market-place for ideas, as the

---

[33] *New Media Markets*, Vol. 14, No. 8, 29 February 1996, p.I.

MMC is already required to do in evaluating cross-ownership of newspapers.

To rely instead on the promulgation of arbitrary regulations means surrendering the ability to apply judgement to each particular set of facts in return for the certainty provided by a formula. Such rules are invariably made obsolete by new technology and new entry almost as quickly as they are promulgated. To avoid reliance on them, it is best to set general parameters which relate to the ultimate objective of cross-media ownership restrictions – the avoidance of concentration.

So it might be appropriate to preclude media acquisitions by any group that already accounts for what is deemed to be an excessive share of audience attention. Under ordinary monopoly rules, a 25 per cent share of a properly measured traditional market would constitute a trigger for an inquiry to ascertain whether the public interest is being harmed. But the media play a special rôle in a democratic society, one that makes it particularly desirable to limit the influence of any one player. So emphasis might be placed on audience shares, rather than on revenues or assets. Any such restriction should recognise that the relevant market is all media. For if each of the media – national newspapers, regional newspapers, magazines, satellite television, terrestrial television, radio – is a separate market, there is no more reason to worry about cross-media ownership than about the acquisition by a newspaper of a cement company.

In sum, we believe that reliance on competition policy, supplemented by an injunction to the competition authorities to take account of the sensitive rôle of the media industries in a democratic society by giving consideration to audience shares, would be the best policy – the one most conducive to reaping the potential benefits of technological and economic changes we know are coming but the nature and timing of which we cannot predict.

ACKNOWLEDGEMENTS

William B. Shew and Irwin M. Stelzer would like to thank Robert Patton of the American Enterprise Institute for his research assistance, and Jane Reed and Andrew Whyte for their help in gathering industry data.

W.B.S.
I.M.S.